small town gardens

small town gardens

Rachel de Thame

Dedication

For my parents, Ghita and Michael Cohen, who, a long time ago, showed a little girl the beauty of plants

Acknowledgements

This book is published to accompany the television series entitled *Small Town Gardens*, first broadcast in 2001 on BBC2.

Series Producer:
Abigail Harvey
Executive Producer: Owen Gay

Published by BBC Worldwide Limited, Woodlands, 80 Wood Lane, London W12 0TT

First published in 2001
Text copyright
© Rachel de Thame, 2001
Garden plans copyright
© BBC 2001, except plan on page 90, copyright
© Douglas Coltart, 2001
The moral right of the author has been asserted.

ISBN 0 563 55180 1

Commisioning Editor:
Vivien Bowler
Project Editor: Khadija Manjlai
Copy-editor: Ruth Baldwin
Art Editor: Lisa Pettibone
Designer: Andrew Barron & Collis Clements Associates

Typeset in Minion and Officina Sans
Printed and bound in France by Imprimerie Pollina s.a.
Colour separations by Pace Digital Limited, Southampton

Previous page: Cool tones and restrained planting bring serenity to a tiny courtyard.

Creating a new series is always a group undertaking, and the *Small Town Gardens* team is second to none, but the impetus, as always, comes from the top.

My thanks to Jane Root for her total commitment to gardening on the BBC, and Owen Gay for igniting the spark that became *Small Town Gardens*; Abigail Harvey, an inspirational series producer and Julia Murkin, the producer, who indefatigably held it all together, headed a team that worked tirelessly on the series; directors Paul O'Connor and David Wheeler; researchers Russell Jordan, Adelle Martins and especially Anna Maynard for her meticulous help in compiling the plant directory for this book; and an excellent group of cameramen, soundmen, editors, office-based researchers and backroom staff.

The series could not have been made without the garden designers who participated so enthusiastically in this adventure in garden design. Thanks to Douglas Coltart, Paul Cooper, Will Giles, Bunny Guinness, Cleve West and Stephen Woodhams; and, of course, the garden owners – Gillian and Julian Herbert, Carol and Richard Hughes, Rose and Nick Painter, Andrea and David Purdie, Ruthanne and Jack Reid and Gill and Chris Short – who all had to contend with muddy footprints, unsociable filming hours and provide gallons of tea.

Thanks also to the following for allowing us to film at their gardens and nurseries: Ian Hamilton, Finlay at Little Sparta, George Anderson at the Royal Botanic Gardens, Edinburgh, the Duke and Duchess of Devonshire at Chatsworth House, John Carter at Rowden Gardens, the Abbey Gardens, Tresco, Angus White at Architectural Plants, Anthony Paul and the Hannah Peschar Sculpture Garden, Beth Chatto, John Humphries at Sutton Place, Marina Christopher and John Coke at Green Farm Plants, Raymond Blanc at Le Manoir aux Quat' Saisons and

Annie Huntington at the Old Rectory Gardens. Finally, thanks also to all the contractors and gardeners – the unsung heroes of the team – who helped us to meet the deadline.

At BBC Worldwide, thanks are due to Robin Wood, Viv Bowler for her patience and encouragement, Khadija Manjlai for guiding me through the book-writing process so painlessly, the meticulous Ruth Baldwin for her copy-editing, Bea Thomas for her impeccable picture research and Andrew Barron, whose design work brought the book to life. Thanks are also due to Jonathan Buckley for his flawless photographer's eye and Dan Welldon for the excellent photographs of the Paisley garden.

Those who offered encouragement from the outset include Rosemary Alexander and Simon Pyle at the English Gardening School, and Tony Laryea and Colette Foster at Catalyst Television, who took a chance on a new girl. Thanks also to Annie Sweetbaum, Hilary Murray-Watts and all at Arlington Enterprises for their unfailing care and commitment; Luigi Bonomi at Sheil Land Associates for his expert guidance on my first foray into book writing; Ghita Cohen, for reading every word of the manuscript, spurring me on when I began to flag and never being too busy to listen to my concerns; Simon Cohen for his valuable contribution to the picture research; and James Gladwin for his much-needed technical support.

And, finally, thanks to my husband, Gerard, for his constant love, support, encouragement and unerring good judgement, and most especially to my children, Lauren and Joseph, for their infinite patience.

contents

introduction

Private gardens cover more than a million acres in this country; most of this vast space is composed not of large rural gardens but small urban plots. From the air it immediately becomes clear just how much of the land in our cities is turned over to tiny gardens. Add up all the little green squares and rectangles, the pots perched on rooftops and balconies, and you have a true picture of the strength of our national obsession – and I don't mean football. If Napoleon were describing our nation today, he'd have to substitute the word 'gardeners' for 'shopkeepers'.

Those of us who live willingly or otherwise in towns and cities are no less keen than country folk to have our own patch of green. In fact, such is the strength of the desire to grow plants and humanize urban spaces by surrounding ourselves with living things that we cram them into every available nook and cranny. The most inhospitable basement wells in front of old terraced houses receive almost no light, yet we won't give up trying to make something grow, and rightly so. If that is your only outdoor space, you should make the best of it, and you can be assured there is something that will thrive there, however difficult the conditions.

Eighty per cent of gardeners have plots that are less than 18m (60ft) long, with town gardens being even smaller. Yet the traditional gardening press seems to give a disproportionate amount of attention to large rural gardens with acres of bowling-green lawn and swathes of herbaceous perennials billowing in endless borders. It's all very lovely, and we can certainly take inspiration from such gardens, but what we need is information relevant to our own modest back yards. There are no restrictions as to what you can do in a small city garden, only perceived restrictions. If you want to devote the space to vegetables, go ahead. If you yearn to recreate the Amazon jungle on a housing estate, go for it.

Small spaces, far from being a problem, can actually prove advantageous. Having a limited area forces you to hone the design, to get rid of distracting elements and consider carefully practical aspects such as storage, lighting and irrigation. Gardeners with small plots quickly become adept at weeding out plants that aren't earning their keep, and moving or pruning others to suit the specific conditions. In a tiny garden you can't afford to have areas that look tatty or past their best; being fussy about the plants you buy and where you place them makes you a very selective shopper.

The most adventurous steps in domestic garden design often occur in city gardens, with cutting-edge modern and minimalist gardens becoming increasingly popular with ordinary homeowners. Whether this is

because town dwellers are more adventurous or because it's harder to break away from traditional styles in the country is debatable, but size restrictions can actually help to create a really strong design statement. Confined by a clear boundary, the design cannot become diluted, as is often the case in larger gardens through simply having a large space that needs filling, or an ancient rockery, border or topiary hedge that no one dare touch.

The majority of people living in cities are doing so, I'm pleased to say, because they want to. Towns are invigorating places in which to dwell and bring up children. Watching people on the move in cities that never sleep and revelling in the buzz that pervades modern urban spaces are often the reasons why people enjoy living in them. If you find you're trying to block it all out, perhaps you should consider a move. It is a

misconception that towns and gardens are incompatible; on the contrary, having a bit of green space, somewhere to escape from the inevitable pressures that go with urban living, can be crucial to our quality of life.

Most of us will never own a large garden, and many of us choose to remain in the city all our life. Small urban plots are the gardening reality for the majority of us. This book recognizes that fact, and aims to show that having this sort of garden should not be regarded as a disadvantage. With careful planning and clever design, city gardens can outdo the rural equivalents in originality and ingenuity. Above all, this book is a celebration of small town gardens and the joy they give to millions of gardeners and non-gardeners alike.

Above left: Lushly planted
evergreens bring a touch
of the exotic to the heart
of the city.

Above right: Simplicity
and symmetry combine
to create a sleekly modern
style that is perfectly
suited to a small
urban garden.

Opposite left: An eclectic
mixture of objects brings
individuality to a corner
with a seaside theme.

Opposite middle:
Architectural plants
heightened with bright
colour are packed into this
small space.

Opposite right: Gently
flowing water brings a
sense of calm to a Japanese-
influenced garden.

plotting *and* planning

Starting work on a new garden, or changing the style of an existing one is an exciting

time. Small town plots have just as much potential as large country gardens and can

be anything you want them to be; many of the most interesting developments in

garden design are happening in unlikely urban environments. The first step is to

decide on a look that's right for you, your family and your lifestyle, and then put it

into practice. Lack of space need not restrict your imagination, so make bold choices

and you'll reap the benefits in the future.

Left: Limiting the colour palette to shades of green can bring coherence to a small space.

Opposite: The restraint shown in this formal geometric design results in an intensely satisfying garden, proving that less is indeed more.

Take a cool hard look at your garden. Is it the best it could be? Is it what you want? Could it be improved? Many of us delay doing something about the exterior space until the interior is finished, but the effort and expense of improving the garden is disproportionate to the amount of pleasure we then get from using it. Tackling your outside space should not be an afterthought; it's well known that a beautiful garden is a major factor in helping to sell a property, as well as adding considerably to the value of a house or flat. It's a fact that good gardens get noticed and add to our quality of life.

Having decided to make improvements, the starting point is to assess your garden carefully. Which direction does it face? Is there any area that gets full sun or is it all in permanent shade? Are there any existing trees and – unless they are protected, in which case you need permission in order to touch them – are they contributing anything to the garden? If there are none, would adding a tree improve the garden? Think long term; tiny saplings can quickly cast a lot of shade. There are many more questions you need to answer: is the garden overlooked? Could something be done to improve your privacy? What about storage, a greenhouse, a water feature, growing vegetables? Look critically at the boundaries, the garden floor, and the access into the garden from the house.

Your garden can be anything you want it to be, and deciding on a style is one of the best parts of planning a new garden. If you yearn for tropical climes but live in, say, the northern part of the UK, you can still have an exotic feel to the garden. Landlocked seaside lovers can bring a taste of marine life to the city, and a corner of Japan can come to you, complete with bamboo, bonsai and boulders, wherever you live. Whether you have a penchant for traditional soft curves, formal box parterres or concrete and sleek lines, it can all be achieved in a small town garden.

Of course there are practicalities to consider. Before doing anything else, make a list of what you actually need, then move on to what you really want. If you have three boys under five, it will frustrate everybody if your minimalist garden has nowhere to store dayglo plastic cars, bikes and footballs. We all reach an age when stooping to deal with weeds becomes more difficult, so raised beds and low-maintenance planting are the perfect answer. There are solutions to most problems, without having to compromise the look of the garden; what's needed is clever design.

Not all of us can call on the services of a garden designer, though we can draw inspiration from seeing examples of their work. With thought and imagination we can do a lot to improve our own gardens. Be realistic about your budget and cut your coat

to fit your cloth. Where possible, employ the services of professionals to deal with the aspects of remaking the garden that you find daunting; many garden landscaping companies offer a design service. However, there is a surprising amount that can be done by keen, fit and enthusiastic amateurs. Use one of the new three-dimensional computer programs to help you visualize your design, or work on paper; there are many good books on garden design to help you. When in doubt, the best approach is to keep it simple.

Once you've chosen a style, taken careful measurements and drawn up a plan, the next step will be to clear the garden. It's liberating to get rid of outdoor clutter: just as clearing out an interior boxroom filled with junk can be a cathartic experience, so can removing a tired lawn or overgrown shrubs from the garden. Being unsentimental about the garden requires a different way of thinking. If you're used to saving any plant that shows the smallest sign of being alive, it will be hard to throw out those that are perfectly healthy but are no longer right for the garden. By all means incorporate anything that could work in a different position – even mature shrubs can recover from a move if it is done carefully – then give away what you cannot use. Be aware that the design will be compromised if you attempt to salvage everything.

Installing the hard landscaping elements of the garden can be both terrifying and exciting. When all around you is a sea of mud, it's tempting to wonder why you ever embarked on such a project and suddenly you miss that scrappy bit of weedy turf you called a lawn. Forge ahead, however; this part of the overhaul imperceptibly reaches a turning point when you can really see the design beginning to emerge. Be flexible – this is the stage when changes can still be made, and you never know what obstacles or advantages you may discover while work is in progress.

With the bones of the garden in place, it's time to flesh it out. For me the most worthwhile stage of the transformation is getting the plants in, but some groundwork needs to be done to give them the best possible chance in life. Any form of building work will have a detrimental effect on the structure of the soil, and the gardens of newly built houses often have rubble barely concealed just beneath the surface. You may be forced to skim off soil that has been badly contaminated with cement mixture and other detritus, and import fresh topsoil from elsewhere. Buy from a reliable supplier and, if possible, pay them a visit first to see exactly what you're getting.

Even if your existing soil is worth keeping, it will still benefit hugely from an injection of goodness. Work in plenty of organic material in the form of well-rotted farmyard manure –

Left: The flower-filled
borders and gentle curves
of traditional garden style
can soften the hard lines
of the urban environment.

which can be bought ready-bagged from garden centres – or good garden compost. Many town gardens have heavy clay soil which, though fertile, is stiff and sticky in the winter and parched and cracked in summer. Improve the drainage by incorporating horticultural grit with the manure or compost. Improving the soil structure is a long-term investment; putting in expensive plants without preparing the ground properly first could be a costly mistake.

Once you're ready to start planting, get the big structural plants in first. When drawing up the plan of the garden, you will probably have decided on their final positions, but the smaller plants may still need to be arranged. Most designers use some sort of block planting technique, placing several plants of the same type together to create drifts or geometric chunks for maximum effect. Avoid bitty

planting with dozens of different varieties packed together. It's often a case of less is more. Lay out all the plants in their positions before planting and move things around until they look right. Remember to stand back from large plants once you've dropped them into the planting hole to check that they're facing the right way: many individual specimens have a definite front and back.

Some fixed accessories, such as recessed lighting and water features, will have gone in at the building stage. The fun part – dressing the garden – adds finishing touches, such as containers, furniture and movable lights, and is much like arranging objects in the home. Choose well-made items that add to the overall design statement. Don't feel you have to fill every corner of the garden. The space around things is often just as important in terms of visual success.

One of the biggest bonuses of a small plot is that it's not unrealistic or too expensive to have a change when you fancy something completely different. Fashions move on in garden design as in everything else. Think of the garden as a constantly evolving space; living plants never remain the same, so neither does the look of a garden. You should play an active part in altering your outdoor space. Put your own imprint on it and make it something unique that reflects your tastes and the way in which you live today.

Above left: A patchwork of contrasting gravels, sempervivums and *Solierolia solierolii* (mind-your-own-business) add interest to the garden floor.

Above right: Incorporating the needs of children is what family gardens are all about.

Opposite left: Children will love quirky features such as these pod chairs, but water is strictly for older kids.

Opposite middle: A mulch of coloured glass beads sets off a collection of contrasting grasses to perfection.

Opposite right: Swirls of pebbles introduce shape and texture underfoot.

the **family garden**

Gardens are for families and the best spaces fulfil the needs of parents and children.

Adults need somewhere to relax, entertain friends and indulge a love of gardening. Kids,

from toddlers to teenagers, descrve a flexible space in which to play in safety and allow

their imagination full rein. It's a lot to pack in. Combining the needs of the whole family

in a restricted space is not easy, but with planning and clever design you can create a

beautiful garden from a potential battlefield.

Modern family life is hectic; both parents may be working and time spent together as a family is precious. Ensuring the garden is a family-friendly space that works for everyone will help us enjoy to the full our time with the children. Small children and small gardens are not the most compatible combination; kids need space to run around and expend some of that boundless energy, and space is the one thing lacking in small gardens. This doesn't mean that the majority of children's other needs cannot be met in a small plot, and on the plus side, gardens designed with children in mind are usually fun, friendly spaces. Keep a sense of humour and use clever design solutions to make the garden a success for the entire family.

Some of my best memories as a parent are of events that have happened in our city garden: the howls of laughter and hysterical whoops as the children run through a sprinkler on a hot day; their uncontrollable giggles when pretending not to want to get 'caught' by the hose while fully dressed. I can still picture my children in straw hats, sitting drawing in the shade, finding that frogs had invaded the outsize paddling pool, and enjoying birthday parties that rapidly got out of control. These are the things that make having a garden such a valuable part of life. To exclude our children from enjoying to the full the outdoor space, however small, is to deny pleasure to them and to us.

The problems arise when you crave a super-smart minimalist garden. Although you dearly love your children, how can you combine the two when they're so clearly at odds? There are really two ways to approach this mismatch. You could turn over the garden completely to the needs of your young family when they need it most; after all, in retrospect the years of swinging on a rope and making perfume from your prize blooms are all too fleeting. Some of the purpose-built play structures are attractive enough, and even better when custom made. Playhouses, sandpits, climbing frames, goalposts, swings and slides don't have to be made from garish plastic, and can all be dismantled once they're outgrown. Well-designed storage is a necessity for large items, such as bikes and paddling pools. Once the children reach a certain age (often signalled by a desire to hide in their bedrooms day and night with their friends), it's time to get rid of all the childish clutter and start again, this time to please yourself.

Alternatively, if you cannot wait that long to get your garden back, you will have to share it from the start. Employ ingenious methods to combine the needs of adults and children, and find ways to conceal all the practical stuff that goes with a modern childhood. Again, the key to success lies in providing sufficient storage: if it's easy at the end of the day to sweep away the detritus of play, there will be fewer areas of contention. Gardens should feed a child's

Opposite: Vivid colours, eye-catching plants, child-friendly accessories and a soft play surface combine to make a stimulating space for the very young.

Right: A deep layer of bark chippings provides a soft surface beneath this shady play area.

Below: The paraphernalia of play can be successfully incorporated into the smallest spaces; here, it forms the basis of the entire design.

imagination, and hide-and-seek can be played in the smallest spaces if there are 'secret' corners or large shrubs to conceal a little person. When incorporating pieces of sculpture or large structures, try to choose items that could metamorphose in a child's mind to become the deck of a ship, a car, or a fairy castle.

Wherever possible, include water in the design. Choose a more naturalistic pond to encourage wildlife; you'll find that frogs and damselflies will appear from nowhere overnight. In a modern space, imaginative ways with flowing water can fascinate children, but do bear in mind that kids love to get wet. How will the design of the feature stand up to the wear and tear of children's play and, above all, is it safe?

Planting should also be child-friendly. A surprising number of plants are highly poisonous, and are best avoided while children are at the stage when everything goes into their mouths. Laburnum, aconitum and yew are all toxic. Check with your nurseyman when buying plants that might tempt small fingers and explain to your children that birds can safely eat red berries that will give *them* a bad tummy ache. A lawn is undoubtedly the most comfortable play surface, but once the games become more boisterous and the tricycles are swapped for mountain bikes, it will need a fastidious gardener to keep it looking good. Choose brightly coloured, scented and even humorous plants to stimulate all the children's senses. Popping open the mouths of snapdragons and stroking the kitten-soft leaves of *Stachys lanata* can keep a child happy for hours. Wherever you can, give children a small corner of the garden to grow their own plants: the excitement of watching a seed germinate, develop and finally flower has instilled a love of plants and gardens in generations of youngsters. It's an experience that city-dwelling children shouldn't be denied.

a family garden
designed by **Cleve West**

A larger-than-average town garden with stately, mature trees and dappled shade, this plot sounded idyllic on paper; the reality was more of a battlefield. The owners of this garden in Harborne on the outskirts of Birmingham barely used the majority of their leafy exterior, and were scared to venture beyond the boundaries of the tiny patio outside the back door. It wasn't a bad case of agoraphobia that prevented them from enjoying the garden to the full, but fear of being hit by a football in full flight, or some other low-flying missile. The owners' four young sons and their friends had turned the garden into a scene from *The Lord of the Flies*.

The garden was long and rectangular with a pleasant prospect and not badly overlooked by the neighbours' windows. There were several existing large trees, with spreading canopies overhanging the plot. North-facing, this garden was blessed with only intermittent periods of sunshine and, for the most part, the space was in dappled or full shade. This is a problem only if you crave the sun and are desperate to grow sun-loving plants. In many ways the garden – though unstructured – certainly had plenty of potential.

The vast majority of the space was entirely taken up by a worn and patchy lawn, which was strewn with bikes and assorted footballs. Some attempt had been made to introduce a variety of plants, but many were unsuitable for the shady conditions and others were languishing in pots. Towards the rear of the garden was an old, neglected climbing-frame. At the end

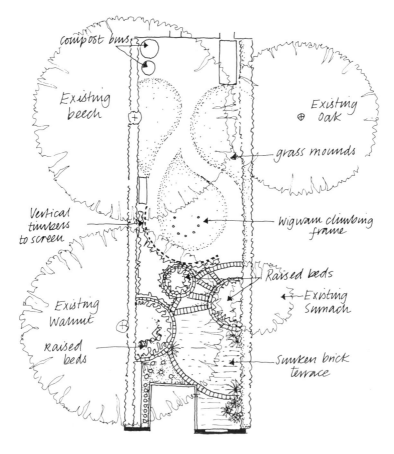

compost bins:3

Existing beech

Existing Oak

grass mounds

Vertical timbers to screen

Wigwam climbing frame

Raised beds

Existing Sumach

Existing Walnut

raised beds

sunken brick terrace

Left: A simple but highly practical timber frame ensures the children's bikes stay off the lawn.

Opposite: Sound and movement are introduced in the form of a child-safe water feature.

nearest the house an extremely cramped patio area sat directly outside the doors of the glazed kitchen extension. For a reasonably sized garden, there was little space to sit or to entertain, few areas suitable for planting and insufficient storage for the ever-expanding belongings of four lively lads.

This project needed a designer with vision – someone who could bring out the potential in a promising site while dealing effectively with the practical problems. Enter multi-award-winning Cleve West (see Designers' Biographies, page 122), one of our most innovative young designers, renowned for his imaginative and solidly built gardens. Cleve frequently collaborates with his business partner, Johnny Woodford, to create atmospheric, uncluttered spaces, incorporating spectacular organic sculptures. He likes his gardens to have a sense of quiet strength and permanence, to feel as if they have been there for some time and are simply continuing to evolve.

Having spent time chatting to the owners, getting to know what their priorities were, and watching their children kick a ball about, Cleve – a keen football fan himself – measured up carefully before heading back to his studio to get his ideas down on paper. The resulting design worked with the existing overhanging trees to create a garden that would instantly become at one with its

surroundings. Cleve chose to work with curved shapes, interlocking a series of circles and gently sweeping lines. He got rid of the dull flat space and divided the garden into two main areas, using different levels to add structural variety. The section nearest to the house was to become a sunken terrace, with plenty of space for the adults to sit out, enjoy the garden and entertain without being terrorized by the kids. This area was much larger than the original patio, taking up more than one-third of the garden. A tall physical barrier would divide this part of the plot from a generous area of lawn, which would fill the remainder of the garden. The design incorporated plenty of large beds for planting, to satisfy the owners' desire to grow a much wider selection of plants. While Cleve discussed the plan with his clients, footballs thwacked rythmically into the plants covering the fence, emphasizing the need to move fast to regain some territory.

Work began as soon as possible. While the plot was being cleared, several of the existing shade-loving plants were salvaged. They were potted up until they could be repositioned in the finished garden. The entire plot was then landscaped to form gentle undulating mounds beneath the lawn. By getting away from a traditional flat bowling-green swathe, Cleve made the lawn more interesting for imaginative play. The area nearest the house was excavated to make a clear distinction

between the lower sunken terrace and the grass area beyond. These two levels were to be linked by a series of wide curved steps. Once the surface of the ground had been scooped and moulded to fit Cleve's design, the hard landscaping could begin. A master of grounded, solid gardens, Cleve likes to use heavy materials and had chosen a mixture of granite setts, bricks – some of them recycled – and timber. The terrace was paved using red bricks in a simple herringbone design. This was edged with larger blue engineering bricks, which followed the curve of the terrace's rounded shape. The walls of the circular raised beds were built with row upon row of heavy granite setts. Each row was simply bedded on to a layer of soil. No mortar was needed to secure them; the weight of the setts themselves was sufficient to compact the soil and make the structure really solid. Each new row of setts was slightly set back from those in the row below, so the walls gently tapered inwards as they ascended. Occasionally Cleve left a gap in the wall, in which to plant a fern or some ivy.

The beds slowly reached the required height, but Cleve had a couple of changes in mind. On one side of the garden the heights were looking too uniform, so he decided that another tier should be added to the larger bed. The other change was a little more drastic. Since finalizing the design Cleve had felt it could be improved upon by introducing

water into the garden. After a quick discussion with the owners – though the work was now well under way – it was agreed to include water in the design. The circular bed in the prime position near the steps was soon adapted to become a unique water feature.

This was to be a covered feature; the constant drop of foliage from the surrounding trees would have resulted in many hours being spent collecting leaves from the surface of even a small area of open water. A large, circular, pre-fabricated plastic pool was hidden below the rim of the raised bed. It contained the water and an electric pump, and was covered with metal mesh. This mesh supported the centrepiece – a large coil of heavy rusted chain, wound into a ball around a simple fountain-head and placed in the middle of the grid. Around the chain ball concentric circles of gravel and *Soleirolia soleirolii* (commonly known as mind-your-own-business) rayed from the centre out to the edge of the bed. The mixture of colours – the dark grey of the gravel, the speckled orange of the rusty chain and the vivid green of the planting – were a subtle but stunning combination.

When the water was turned on, it bubbled gently through the top of the ball, bringing the restful sound of babbling water to the terrace. Whether Cleve intended a surrealist pun on the words 'ball and chain' when he

Left: Coils of rusted chain glisten on a bed of *Soleirolia soleirolii* and gun-metal-grey gravel.

During Cleve's initial meeting with the owners, they had joked that what was needed was a 'Berlin Wall' between them and the more raucous children's activities. Cleve took them at their word. To everyone's astonishment enormously tall telegraph poles began to appear and were fixed on their ends one after the other about 12 cm (5 in) apart, like sentries on guard. The introduction of a feature of this scale is always something of a shock, but Cleve persevered, convinced that this bold wall of poles would tie the whole design together. The wall continued from one side of the garden to the point at which the steps reached the lawn. Once in place the poles were stained matt black and their tops were cut to size; they now tapered down in a swooping curve towards the centre and up again slightly on the other side. As well as protecting other garden users from projectiles, this feature immediately became a piece of sculpture on the grand scale when viewed from a distance. And if you look at the garden through the gaps between the poles as you walk slowly by, the effect is like watching the flickering frames of an old silent movie.

After the existing hedges were tidied up, turf was laid over the newly shaped upper section of the garden, sweeping over the large central mound and down again into the surrounding 'valley'. Another sculptural structure was constructed atop the mound. This was a hybrid of different ideas and inspirations.

came up with this design is unclear, but the result is simple, witty and – almost perversely – very soothing.

The steps linking the two levels of the garden were built while Cleve was away from the site. On his return, he found a problem. Although beautifully made, the treads of each step had been carefully covered in crazy paving. At times a designer has to become a diplomat. Cleve tactfully pointed out to the man who had just constructed the steps that the crazy paving was beautifully done, but completely out of character with the rest of the garden and not part of the original design. It would have to go. To Cleve's relief, the man immediately agreed that he didn't like it either, and happily started to lever up the broken slabs. Disaster averted, the treads could now be filled with granite setts, as per the original spec.

Solid poles were rammed into the ground in a semi-circle and tied together at the top to form an open-sided wigwam. At the apex a large, decorative coil of rope was nailed down, echoing the shape of the ball of chain on the water feature. Swags of the same rope were then strung between the poles. This structure could be climbed like a climbing-frame; it could be the rigging of a ship, a spider's web, a goalpost or, of course, a wigwam. Rather spookily, Cleve later found out that some of the family's ancestors were Native Americans.

With the garden construction complete, the planting could begin. The soil in the raised beds was extremely dry and sandy. It needed beefing up with plenty of organic material, so lashings of compost and well-rotted manure were added to improve the soil structure and help retain moisture. Cleve's design called for large swathes of single-variety planting – nothing fussy in this garden. To give height to the back of a bed, he planted a leycesteria with deep reddish-purple bracts. A sweep of *Rodgersia aesculifolia* on one side of the terrace was mirrored on the other by a group of *Acanthus spinosus* with large glossy leaves. Some of the salvaged plants found new homes: our native fern *Dryopteris filix-mas*, which is a tough customer, was planted in the dry shade nearest the house, and a *Carex pendula* was given pride of place next to the water feature. Towering, pure white *Agapanthus africanus* 'Albus' were planted in

tall containers and placed on the terrace. Cleve very much hoped that the new garden would inspire the owners, already on the verge of becoming keen gardeners, to take up the trowel and add to the planting as they became more confident. This garden is certainly an ideal environment for bulbs, many of which would thrive in the semi-shady conditions.

The moment the family were able to start using the garden, they began to make it their own. Despite the highly innovative design details, this garden instantly felt comfortable. It is rare for a newly built garden to acquire such atmosphere and a real sense of permanence so quickly. Above all, Cleve's design succeeds in keeping all the family members happy. The adults can enjoy relative peace and quiet and absolute protection from flying objects. A long, low wall, constructed from sleepers and placed along the boundary on one side of the terrace, provides informal seating for entertaining. The owners plan to do plenty of this now that plates and glasses are no longer in constant danger of being knocked over, while the children can play as wildly as they please, without constant censure from their parents.

From an overgrown shady plot – the stage for many scenes of family strife – Cleve has created an imaginative yet calm garden that feels solid enough to last for ever.

dealing *with* shade

Shady gardens, like the one in the case study, are usually seen as a problem, but in many respects they can be a blessing. Once you accept the limitations on the range of plants you can grow and have come to terms with losing the real sun-lovers, you can appreciate the benefits. Gardens have a completely different atmosphere in the shade. Their gentle ambience and total absence of garish flower colour create elegant and peaceful spaces, and on those – albeit rare – sweltering summer days you'll appreciate the cooler air.

Losing out on a full quota of sunshine doesn't mean the garden will look boring. There is a wonderful range of plants that insists on shady places in order to do well. Many shrubs grow in woodland conditions in nature and will thrive if you can create a similar environment in your shady garden. Some of the best mid-height plants with strong structural leaf shapes – such

as Rodgersias and Rheums – are also shade-lovers; these look their best planted *en masse* to fill the mid-storey. Beneath them perennials, such as *Helleborus orientalis*, *Geranium phaeum* and a host of hostas and ferns, thrive. Many bulbs are also happiest in shady spots, giving a wealth of blooms throughout the year. The flowers of shade-loving plants tend to be subtle, but are no less lovely for that. These soft, pale tones glow in low light levels, shimmering in a rich sea of contrasting foliage.

Determine the type of shade in your own garden before you purchase a single plant. If you have a courtyard garden enclosed on all sides, or a basement lower than street level, it's most likely in full shade. Gardens in the lee of a large tree will be subjected to dry shade, one of the most difficult conditions to deal with. The roots of a mature tree are thirsty and hungry, and will compete for available moisture and nutrients. Rain may have trouble filtering through a dense canopy, as will sunlight. Lawns will have difficulty surviving these conditions, but there are many plants that will do surprisingly well; it's just a question of making a considered choice.

Smaller trees often result in dappled shade. This type of shade is much easier to deal with and enlarges considerably the range of suitable plants. Your garden may have semi-shade conditions, with full sun for part of the day before it disappears entirely behind your house

or use shiny metallic materials. Mirrors can also be used to brighten a dark corner. What you choose to put on the garden floor can make a huge difference to a shady garden. Pale Portland stone, light-coloured gravel and galvanized metal will instantly lift the area and are perfect for courtyard gardens. It may be best, however, to avoid using pale gravel under large trees – it soon becomes covered in green moss or algae, which is difficult to remove. Plants with variegated leaves will also lift dark areas. A surprising number tolerate low light conditions. *Euonymus fortunei* 'Silver Queen' is a perfect, low-growing evergreen for the front of a border, and there are numberous hostas that will fit the bill.

It's impossible to reorientate your garden, and there is little you can do about large trees, so accept what you have to work with. Keep water features small if they are to be positioned near overhanging trees. Removing fallen leaves from the water will soon become a chore.

Most gardeners with shady plots crave the sun-loving plants that will sooner or later fail miserably in their gardens. Far better to grow some of the wonderful plants that will not only survive but thrive in the conditions, and treat the shade as an advantage. It's time to see the light and create something that gardeners with parched sunny plots can only dream of. Lush, verdant and dreamlike, shady gardens have a bright future.

or another building; this is particularly common in town gardens. Such a variance from one extreme to another makes selecting plants a potential minefield. Depending on the amount of full sun, and the time of day in which this occurs, you may even have success with real sun-lovers – silver-leaved beauties, such as lavender, *Helichrysum italicum* and santolina. If the sunny periods are shorter than their optimum growing conditions would dictate, sun-loving perennials will survive but become leggy in their search for better light during the shady part of the day. It's very much a case of choosing varieties that tolerate a bit of both. Trial and error will then narrow the selection down to the best plants for your garden.

A good design trick for a shady plot is to choose bright reflective surfaces to make the most of the available light by bouncing it around the garden. Paint walls in pale colours

the garden floor

One of the main strengths of Cleve's design for the family garden in Harborne was his imaginative use of landscaping materials. The combination of brickwork and granite setts formed the backbone of the design. Yet what we put on the garden floor is often the most neglected part of the garden. Time and money are lavished on plants, pots and water features, while what lies beneath our feet is ignored.

Look at any photograph of an attractive small garden, then cover the ground space with your hand: you'll find that in most cases the floor is what holds the entire design together. The garden floor is often the largest single element in a garden. For a design to be successful as a whole, you need to start with the base level before you can work upwards. What you choose is likely to require a considerable financial investment and will affect the whole atmosphere of the garden. Don't rush to make a decision. Do your research first, visit other gardens to see what works and scour the latest magazines and design books. Your choice will probably be with you for a while.

Just a few years ago, the number of options in garden surface materials was limited. There was the obvious lawn, stone slabs (if you were lucky), concrete paving stones (usually in the form of crazy paving), brick and gravel. Today things couldn't be more different. Innovation

in garden flooring has made it the most exciting growth area in the world of garden design. For every style and theme of garden there is something to go on the ground that will enhance that particular space, and the range is expanding all the time.

Many of us like the feel of something soft underfoot that is also a safe play surface for children. Lawns have had a bad press recently, and it's true that in small city gardens they're not always the best choice. All too often shady town gardens are held hostage to a tiny scrap of tatty old turf. Grass will never grow successfully in the shade, particularly the dry shade found under the crown of large trees or right next to shade-making buildings. If your garden has similar conditions, don't bother trying to grow a lawn. It's rare to find a small town garden in full sun, but many are blessed with sun for at least part of the day and these plots are more likely to sustain a reasonable patch of grass.

If you do decide to have all or part of the garden turfed, keeping the shape simple is invariably the best plan. Fiddly convoluted shapes are much too fussy in a large garden and look ridiculous in a small one. Choose a simple oval in informal gardens, and rectangular shapes where the design is symmetrical. It's a misconception that lawns look inappropriate in a modern design – they can be incorporated in the most minimalist

Opposite: Panels of timber decking give this garden a strong geometric structure, softened by a subtly toned woodstain and an abundance of foliage plants.

Right: Illuminated glass blocks inset into a lawn make a change from traditional paviours, and look stunning after dark.

garden very successfully, particularly when the rest of the planting is spare. Lawns don't always have to be curved: straight-sided shapes often work best in an urban environment.

Careful ground preparation and using the correct grass mix are the keys to success with lawns. If you have children, forget the bowling-green look and use a tougher, utility-type seed mix or turf. Whether you use seed or buy rolls of turf will depend on your budget and how quickly you need to get the job done. Seed is much cheaper and you can be sure of exactly what you're getting, but you may not be able to use the lawn properly for at least five months. Turf certainly looks good almost immediately, but it too needs a couple of months to come fully into growth. Do buy turf from a reputable supplier and, if possible, ask to see it first: it's all too easy to end up with a bit of weedy meadow.

Having a lawn doesn't preclude the use of other materials. Most designs will incorporate a terrace, steps or a path. But in many circumstances a lawn simply isn't suitable; far better to choose a hard landscaping surface. Here there need be no limit to your creativity and in a small space you can revel in making a real statement with the garden floor. From the most traditional-looking design to cutting-edge modernity, there is a surface for every garden.

Stone, granite and gravel are endlessly practical, adaptable and the longest-lasting materials. Brick is still one of the most flexible choices, with a range of sizes and colours available. Concrete has taken on a new image and looks fantastic in modern gardens. Some of the new, reconstituted stone products make complex designs with paving and cobbles simplicity itself to construct, and not beyond the average pocket. Timber gives instant warmth and texture to a garden and is now no longer restricted to simple strip decking. The most exciting development is the widening range of materials that designers are using. Plastic and rubber surfaces, once strictly for commercial use, are finding their way into the domestic garden. Galvanized metal and crushed glass are reflective surfaces that bring maximum light into dark city gardens.

With so many options, it's getting harder to make a choice, and sometimes the answer is to use a couple of different surfaces. Combining two or more contrasting materials is all part of the art of garden creativity. But avoid the temptation to use a bit of everything. In a small garden things can quickly look cluttered; as in all areas of design, a little goes a long way.

Above left: Strong shapes, bold colours and an exciting use of materials combine to great effect.

Above right: The soft fronds of grasses and sedums are silhouetted against a movable screen.

Opposite left: A geometric grid of contrasting flooring materials is softened by an ethereal collection of grasses.

Opposite right: Pared-down style calls for pared-down lighting.

the **modern garden**

Small spaces need big ideas, and town gardens lend themselves extremely well to modern style. A clean, minimalist approach suits the cityscape. Straight lines, geometric shapes and the use of metal, glass and concrete echo and enhance the shapes we see all around us. We've become braver in our interior design. Now it's time to shake things up outside and create an unbroken link between the internal and external living space. Revel in the urban – you choose to live in the city because it's colourful and lively, so don't block it out, celebrate it.

Left: The silvery metallic
sheen of a light fitting
that is small, simple and
stunning.

Opposite: Blurring the
boundaries between the
interior and exterior
unifies the living space,
transforming the garden
into an extra room.

Recent years have seen huge strides in accessible and attainable modern garden design. The groundwork was done in the twentieth century, and now in the twenty-first it is possible for owners of average small plots to chuck out their chintzy gardens and try something new. Small town gardens are especially suited to being at the forefront of this quiet revolution. The smaller scale lends itself particularly well to modern style, and it's somehow less daunting to be brave in an urban environment. Indeed, with the frantic pace of life in the city, it's often beneficial to have a clean, minimalist space in which to escape and unwind. It's worth bearing in mind that some of the latest hi-tech materials are expensive and if you have acres to redesign, you may need a second mortgage.

Now that modern garden design has gone mainstream and is no longer the preserve of the few, even the most traditional gardener should consider a fresh approach. Modern doesn't have to mean empty; it's perfectly possible to have curves, flowers, even a lawn, and retain the sleek lines and calm atmosphere of a modern space. Minimalist designs are more likely to be very sparing with planting and colour, which is a bonus if you have little time to spend tending plants. Making the minimalist style work with small children is tricky, but with clever design it can be done.

Good modern garden design is often linked closely to the house; a seamless transition from one living space to the next has given rise to the outdoor room. Planning your garden so that it functions like another room of the house means that more thought will be given to how you like to spend your time outside. The result is not just a place to grow plants, but a plant-filled environment that fulfils a range of leisure functions for the family and their friends. Plants do not cease to be important in a minimal scheme. On the contrary, when less is more, the plants you choose really have to earn their keep. Single specimens, prominently displayed, attract far more attention than a conglomeration of shrubs.

All too often town gardens are dreary, dark and depressing; a light and airy modern scheme can open up the area, creating the illusion of a larger space. The use of pale colours and reflective surfaces bounces light into those shady corners. Cramped basement and courtyard gardens in particular are greatly improved with this type of treatment. Get rid of your cluttered old garden and enjoy the breath of fresh air that comes with a new approach.

a modern garden
designed by Stephen Woodhams

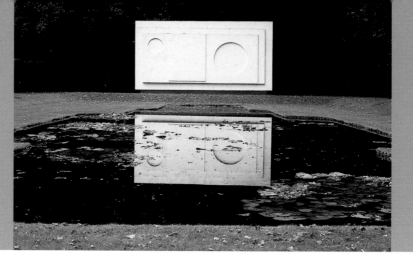

Left: The Ben Nicholson sculpture at Sutton Place in Surrey, Stephen Woodhams's inspirational garden.

Opposite: Link the outdoor space to the interior by unifying colours. Here, the blue of the French doors is reflected in the parasol and walls, and contrasted by the pale blue of the decking.

The owners of this terraced house in Hackney, east London, love the bustle of modern life in the city. They have ripped out walls, stripped off the veneer of age, and dragged their typical Edwardian home firmly into the twenty-first century. When work began on the garden, the interior of the house was still unfinished but well on the way to becoming a sleek, modern, open-plan space, with plenty of metal surfaces, timber floors and seamless expanses of petrol-blue walls. Although modern, the space was approachable, practical and child-friendly. The same couldn't be said of the garden, which was completely overgrown, filled with weeds, a collection of dead or dying plants in pots and a peppering of discarded plastic toys.

This garden was particularly small and irregularly shaped, a rectangle with one straight end that abutted the newly built glazed extension to the house. At the bottom end of the garden, the fence was built at an angle, resulting in one side of the plot being much shorter than the other. On the practical side, this plot would have to work as a family garden, where storage space would be needed for tools and the plethora of toys and bikes that growing toddlers accumulate. There was also a really keen desire to incorporate some sort of safe water feature in the finished garden.

Both the owners work in the visual arts and have a bold approach to design. They wanted to achieve the same sort of strong design

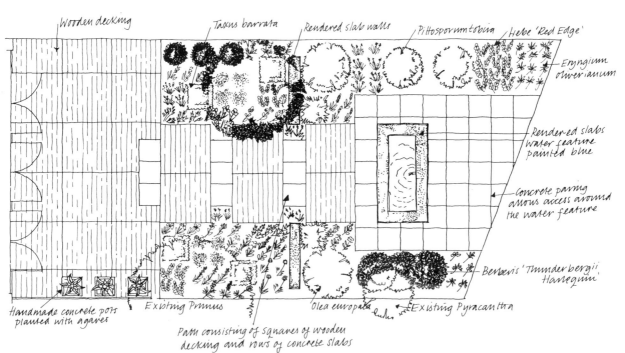

Wooden decking

Taxus baccata

Rendered slab walls

Pittosporum tobira

Hebe 'Red Edge'

Eryngium oliverianum

Rendered slabs water feature painted blue

Concrete paving allows access around the water feature

Berberis 'Thunbergii Harlequin'

Handmade concrete pots planted with agaves

Existing Prunus

Olea europaea

Existing Pyracantha

Path consisting of squares of wooden decking and rows of concrete slabs

Left: *Festuca glauca* nestles at the base of a wall.

Opposite: The satisfying symmetry of the minimalist water feature forms an impressive focal point at the end of the garden.

statement in the garden that they were developing in the house. Apart from an old *Prunus cerasifera* 'Nigra', the crown of which they had previously reduced, there was nothing in the garden they wanted to keep. It's always exciting for a designer to work with brave clients, and we were able to match them with award-winning Stephen Woodhams (see Designers' Biographies, page 122), who is renowned for his sleek, spare and spectacular gardens. Stephen's first visit to the site was productive and positive. Ideas flowed freely among this creative group of people, and Stephen could see from what had been achieved in the house that his clients were open to contemporary ideas. They were also keen to develop their gardening knowledge further, and to grow a wide range of plants. This wasn't to be a minimalist garden in terms of planting.

Having discussed and measured the garden and considered the brief, Stephen went back to the studio to work on the plan. The fruit of his labour was a deceptively simple symmetrical design. He succeeded brilliantly in creating an outdoor room, linked both visually and physically to the new extension. The floor of the garden was to be raised to match exactly the interior floor level, and the petrol-blue paint colour would be continued unbroken on to the exterior surfaces. By creating seamless connections between the inside and the outside spaces, he had magically enlarged both areas. The garden was

to be divided into three sections, using subtle changes in materials at ground level and low rendered walls to give form and structure to the design. All too often small spaces are treated as one area, but by splitting even the tiniest garden into distinct sections it is possible to create the illusion of extra space and achieve a far more interesting result.

The garden was quickly cleared of rubbish and the ground levelled. Carefully chosen hard landscaping materials were installed; simple wooden fence panels with an unusual horizontal construction instantly modernized the boundary abutting the house. Directly outside the extension the first section of the garden was covered with wooden decking in individual rectangular sections. The strips of timber were laid widthways across the garden to exaggerate the size of the space. The decking was given a wash of colour in a soft greyish-blue to look like faded denim and tone with the deeper blue of the main theme colour. The decking narrowed one-third of the way down the garden, becoming a wide path, and the timber panels were interspersed with square concrete paving slabs. These would lead the eye down the length of the garden to the main focal point.

Once the garden floor was complete, the vertical structural elements could be installed. It was extremely exciting to see these structures metamorphose from flat, two-dimensional

details on paper to three-dimensional reality. A pair of low, free-standing walls were built two-thirds of the way down the garden to break up the length of the space. When painted blue, these proved to be one of the most successful aspects of the design, providing structure and a dramatic backdrop to the planting. The main focal point – a third large rectangular wall – was constructed towards the end of the garden. This dominated the plot, gave the illusion that the space was in fact a perfect rectangle and provided a visual full stop. Cleverly, however, the garden did not end at this point: Stephen had concealed behind the wall a simple wooden shed, taking care of all the toys and clutter with one brilliant storage solution.

This wall was more than a strong vertical statement – the addition of a single spout and a slim raised pool to the front of the wall created the much-wanted water feature. The result was minimal in design, powerful in effect and, above all, safe, thanks to a metal grid fixed just centimetres below the water surface. The water was pumped up to the spout before falling again in a single stream back into the pool. During the construction of the water feature a point was reached when the walls had been rendered but remained unpainted. At this stage it looked so attractive that there was some discussion between Stephen and the owners about the possibility of leaving it in its raw state rather than painting it as he had planned. As Stephen

explained, 'One has, of course, to be open to the possibility of changing the design from time to time – you never know what ideas can crop up during the work.' But in this instance he stuck to his guns, feeling that his original instincts were correct, and the results show how that clarity of vision can make the difference between so-so and stunning.

With the hard landscaping completed, the planting could begin. In addition to the prunus, Stephen had decided to retain a mature pyracantha towards the rear of the garden. In early autumn the brilliant orange berries would provide a stunning contrast to the petrol-blue walls. He felt that some height was also needed on the opposite side of the garden, to balance the existing tree, and a semi-mature *Acer japonica*, with complementary plummy-coloured foliage, was the first plant to go in. Vertical accents were also provided by a pair of slender olive trees. These specimens had not been standardized to leave bare trunks, but retained their feathered lower branches, which appeared right from the base. Though not hardy in exposed areas, these should be perfectly happy in a sheltered London town garden. Their silvered leaves catch the light as they twirl in the slightest breeze, and they may even produce olives.

Other architectural plants soon followed. A pair of matching bamboos – *Fargesia*

Left: A trio of *Agave america* in tall containers create a strong vertical accent, and raise the spiky leaves out of the reach of children.

Opposite: An array of foliage shapes and textures and a palette of greens contrast with the intense blue of the walls.

murieliae 'Simba' – were placed just behind the two low walls, the stems arching gracefully into view and showing off to perfection the bright green foliage against the vivid blue paintwork. Several purple-leaved *Berberis thunbergii* 'Harlequin', with wine-red foliage speckled with cream, were added to tone with the acer and provide some height next to the fence. Stephen's planting scheme for the beds flanking the wide central path followed the geometric theme of the garden as a whole. A diverse range of plants was planted in blocks of varying heights and textures. This avoided uniformity and was unconventional in not banking the plants from highest at the back of the bed to lowest at the front.

Solid cubes of box contrasted with silvery domes of *Santolina chamaecyparissus* 'Lambrook Silver' and the strappy foliage of *Iris sibirica* 'Silver Edge'. Foliage colour ranged from deep plums and dark greens to vivid lime-green and silver-grey, and with the addition of *Helichrysum italicum* subsp. *serotinum* (the curry plant) and *Artemisia* 'Powis Castle' the garden will always be scented. Subtle flower colour in soft blues, mauves and purple – toning with the blue walls – will be provided by the irises and *Lavandula angustifolia* 'Hidcote' in early summer, the spires of *Aconitum carmichaelii* 'Arendsii' and shrubby *Caryopteris* × *clandonensis* 'Worcester Gold' taking over the show in the early autumn. Finally, spiky

hummocks of *Festuca glauca* were placed at the front of the beds, where the concrete slabs cut into the decking.

Finishing touches were added to bring the whole garden together. Beautifully designed lights with metal half-domes punctuated the front of the water feature and the low blue walls. A decorative mulch of paddle stones was spread among the planting, covering any bare soil. This mulch will in future help to prevent weeds from germinating and to retain moisture in the soil, cutting down the need for watering. Stephen then added three identical tall containers to the terrace area, and planted each one with an *Agave americana*. These instantly added a strong architectural element, and were tall enough to prevent their spiny leaves from getting near a small child's eyes.

Stephen's design managed to fulfil exactly the owners' brief and provide that extra special ingredient that shows in the work of a top garden designer. It achieves the near-impossible task of providing a modern but not minimalist garden. This is a wonderfully sleek space, continuing unbroken the design themes developed in the house. But there is still colour and scent, there is a wide range of plants, and there is an awareness of the practical needs of younger members of the family. It is a thoroughly modern garden – and one that works.

Left: The feathered petals of *Tulipa* 'Black Parrot' glow with rich intensity in the spring sunshine.

Opposite: *Papaver somniferum's* crêpe-paper flowers range from pale lilac to deep mauve and this lovely crushed raspberry pink.

against a backdrop of green foliage, create one of the best combinations. The blending of soft pastel shades, so often seen in the blowsy borders of country gardens, is being challenged, particularly in urban gardens, by the use of intense, sometimes clashing, hues. Cities give us the incentive to be brave when putting colours together, and in the increasingly adventurous world of garden design it seems appropriate to be less inhibited in our use of colour.

However, that doesn't mean we should ignore some basic rules. In towns we are surrounded by a kaleidoscope of colour. Bearing in mind that anything visible from the garden constitutes part of the view, it seems wise to consider this when planning our gardens. Much of the background will probably be in the neutral tones of brick, stone, glass and other building materials, as well as the various greens and browns of trees and large shrubs. But your neighbours may have painted their garden shed bright purple, or an overlooking block of flats may have vivid scarlet panels (as does one not far from my own house). These things need to be addressed; ignoring them will not make them disappear from your view, and the best option is to tackle them head on.

If screening isn't possible because of the size and dominance of the feature, it may be best to give in gracefully and design a colour scheme for your own garden that links with,

colour *in* **planting** *and in* **landscape features**

Stephen Woodhams's scheme for the Hackney garden shows how colour can be employed to stunning effect in an exterior space. The use of colour is an intensely personal thing: it can alter mood, stir up strong emotions and be the cause of harmony or disagreements. Most people have very particular ideas about what they like or dislike when it comes to colour in the garden. What makes one person love the combination of orange and pink, when others can barely tolerate anything more colourful than the addition of a little white to highlight a palette of green foliage?

Where colour combinations are concerned, ideas of good taste are no longer so cut and dried. The old adage that 'blue and green should never be seen' is now regularly ignored in garden design. Painted walls and furniture in various shades of blue and bluish-greens are particularly popular and, when placed

Left: Black furniture and accessories stand out against the warmth of a wall painted the colour of ripe papaya flesh.

with groups of vivid tangerine *Tulipa* 'Prinses Irene' followed by clumps of *Iris sibirica* and vibrant orange crocosmias and kniphofias. All will be well until the neighbours paint their pergola pink!

When designing the garden, choose the colour and finish of any hard landscaping elements first. There are several things that might affect your choice. In the smallest spaces tie in the exterior colours to those of the interior of the house. Having a unifying theme to all the living areas will allow a seamless flow as you move from one space into the next, giving the illusion of spaciousness. This method of linking the atmosphere of the room directly to the garden is particularly effective in small modern homes, where we often refer to the garden as an outdoor room. If a chrome and glass kitchen/dining area opens straight on to the garden, re-use those materials, and others that echo them, in the terrace and choose planting to complement them.

A complementary colour doesn't have to be a matching one; as usual, there are alternatives and choices to be made. An exact colour match will create the smoothest and most obvious link to the house; a similar shade or tone of the original will unconsciously link the two. But just as effective is a complete contrast, carefully chosen to bring out the best in the interior shade. Very dark brown, the colour of bitter chocolate, is currently

and is complemented by, the immediate surroundings. Choose plants that echo the colours in the environment around you. These don't have to be identical – it's often better to use subtle tones, blending and softening the overall effect. Pick shrubs with mauve flowers, such as lilacs, to grow near the purple shed, and weave varieties of clematis through the branches to give a second burst of flowers.

If the view is relatively neutral, and the impact won't be too great for your neighbours, you can be brave, choose dominant colours and make your own plot stand out. The power of colour is often in the contrast between two or more. A series of concrete walls, rendered and painted in burnt orange and petrol-blue, juxtaposed one against the other, would be the most fantastic backdrop for evergreen foliage interspersed

Left: The traditional style of a small terrace is enlivened with a lilac wall.

Below left: A white border is the height of restrained elegance.

Below right: The adage 'blue and green should never be seen' doesn't apply to gardens.

fashionable when combined with pale, pepperminty aqua, dark wenge wood veneers and brushed chrome. Plenty of contrasts here, but the strength of the overall combination lies in how the different colours and textures of the materials used in a scheme bring out the best in one another.

Fashion is as fickle in plant colours as it is in anything else. Current trends have included a penchant for black and near-black plants. The black grass *Ophiopogon planiscapus* 'Nigrescens' has sold like hot cakes from garden centres, but needs careful placing and a contrasting background to be seen effectively. *Tulipa* 'Queen of Night' is a deliciously deep shade, as close to a black tulip as we have been able to produce. Both of these examples work brilliantly with the vibrant contrast of acid green euphorbias to set them off perfectly.

In a small space a good way to approach the choice of a colour theme is to choose one dominant colour, then add a couple of tones of that colour and something to act as a sharp contrast. Remember that, whatever else you choose, green foliage will probably be providing the main bulk of colour in the garden. Of course, foliage doesn't come only in green – you could have an area of plants with bronze, red and purple leaves, or an entire section of silver and grey-leaved plants. But most of us like to combine and contrast different foliage colour with a range of greens to add interest and variety to the planting.

lighting:
the
garden
at
night

Lighting can often look out of place in a large expanse of country garden. The restraint imposed by lack of space, however, actually seems to enhance the use of lighting in small city gardens. Look up at the night sky: in large cities the sky is never velvety black as it is out in the country. The warm amber glow is caused by the reflection of millions of lights from towns that never sleep. This is something city dwellers are all familiar with; it takes a visit to the countryside to remind us just how dark the dark can be. Lighting the exterior space at night is something townies are comfortable with, whereas in the country a luminous garden stands out like a sore thumb.

The use of light is a compelling part of modern garden design. City gardens with minimal planting schemes often come to life with just a couple of expertly placed lights. The small town garden and lighting were made for each another. Illuminating the garden will increase the amount of time you'll spend out there: the garden becomes a true extension of the home, with summer days out of doors drifting into balmy nights. With the addition of a heater, this continental café-life need not end with the sudden drop in temperature in the autumn.

But lighting outside needs as much thought as we give it within our homes. Think carefully about the positioning of each light-fitting. Planning on paper is a start, but the placing

may need to be adjusted several times to get exactly the right effect. Don't be tempted to blast the whole area with wattage; subtlety speaks volumes and (as is so often the case) less is frequently more. The aim is not to illuminate the garden to look like the land of the midnight sun, but to create intriguing shadows and soft, mysterious tones, and to highlight special features so that they look even more striking.

The range of different forms of exterior lighting has never been better, with increasingly imaginative alternatives appearing all the time. It's no longer as straightforward as sticking a spotlight on a stake into the ground. There are still plenty of traditional-looking lanterns and porch lights available, but some of the innovations for modern and minimalist garden lighting are among the most thought-provoking and ground-breaking of all areas of contemporary garden design.

Clever use of lighting among the plants can be especially effective. The intense green of illuminated leaves stands out against the night and, when lit from below, the branches of shrubs and small trees create a sculptural tracery as effective as any piece of art. Keep the light source soft; harsh spotlights can create really 'hot' areas and looming dark shadows. Be adventurous: conceal lighting in the crown of trees, wrap tiny fairy lights

around topiary and thread spotlights
through dark corners of the borders to create
hidden areas of magical illumination. You
can also buy coloured lights to shine among
your plants or for use underwater. By all
means give them a try, but the garden can
quickly resemble a stage or film set. Unless
there's a particular effect you're after, you
may prefer not to re-create a *son et lumière*
show in your own garden.

Don't use exterior lighting solely for effect. It's
obviously sensible to make sure steps and
passageways are well lit. Security lighting is
often neglected, but it could make all the
difference in deterring an opportunistic
intruder, and is particularly useful in gardens
outside basement flats.

It's worth mentioning that as a responsible
city dweller you should consider the

neighbours when choosing where to place
lights. Remember that in a small town
environment what we do affects other people
around us. The constant glare of an upward-
facing spotlight could be very unpleasant for
someone on the receiving end, and the cause
of a long-running disagreement. There are
many companies offering a complete lighting
service, planning and installing everything
from start to finish, but at a price.

Alternatively, scan magazines, search the
pages of design books and manufacturers'
catalogues and design your own scheme.
When it comes to the practicalities, however,
it's unwise to try to save money by trying
to do it yourself: electricity is strictly for
the experts.

Of course, lighting up the night isn't solely
reliant on electric power. Solar-powered
lights are becoming increasingly popular and
are much more environmentally friendly,
harnessing the power of the sun and storing
it to use later in the day. Oil lanterns are
long-lasting and give a lovely light. But for
the ultimate romantic atmosphere,
candlelight is still the best. Storm lanterns are
large, producing plenty of light, and practical
when it's a bit breezy. Nightlights dotted
about randomly between the plants, or lined
up like a battalion of tiny torches, are
exquisitely pretty, bringing a fairytale
atmosphere to any garden.

Above left: Water droplets glisten in the sunlight.

Above middle: A sleek, modern fountain is attached to a turquoise blue wall.

Above right: The serenity of a circular pool of still water.

Opposite left: Lead is fashioned into an elegant water feature, topped with a gilded ball.

Opposite middle: Vivid blue walls flank a mirrored waterfall to spectacular effect.

Opposite right: A tiered sculpture forms a tower of flowing water.

the **water garden**

Water is the elixir of life, and incorporating this element into our garden designs brings vitality, movement, sound and serenity. A garden without water can often feel as if something is missing, and it's now so easy to install any sort of feature, from the simplest pond in a pot to a scaled-down version of the extravaganzas at Chatsworth House. Small spaces are no less able to benefit from the positive sensations that water instils, so be bold in your plans and bring its benefits into your own town garden.

Left: Even a small water feature can add movement to the garden.

Opposite: Bubbling water breaks up the still surface of a long narrow rill.

Below left: A tiny courtyard is entirely filled with slate slabs over water.

We are all aware of the importance of water in our life; it is essential to our survival, important to our wellbeing and a crucial part of our recreation. We human beings seem to be drawn to water, perhaps as a result of spending the first nine months of our existence in liquid. Watch babies gurgling in the bath, children splashing in puddles and the scene at the local swimming pool or on the beach. Throughout life water sustains, fascinates and delights us.

Bringing water into a garden often makes it seem complete. For many of us the pleasures of gardening encompass a collection of ideal pursuits – being outside, enjoying the weather or the passing of the seasons, tending plants, entertaining friends, watching our children play or simply relaxing – and water enhances most of these experiences. Water is also extremely sensuous: who can resist the

temptation to draw their hand through the silken surface of a still pool?

Small gardens are perfectly suited to the introduction of water. Often the whole design can be planned around water. But even if you install just the simplest of water features in a pot, you can enjoy watching the light playing on the surface, try a couple of the wide selection of aquatic plants and encourage more wildlife into your patch.

There are many artists working with water to create sculptures that shimmer with its movement, but you can produce similar effects in your own garden. Build a free-standing mirrored wall with a concealed length of plastic pipe fixed to the top edge. The resulting sheets of water slipping down the glassy surface can be hypnotic to watch. Pump water through a group of slender hollow tubes cut off at different levels like organ pipes and it will gently flow back down the sides, creating a quiet but effective display.

Sometimes the gentlest features are the most effective. Still pools bring serenity and a calming atmosphere into a garden, and work particularly well in formal or symmetrical spaces, whether traditional or modern in style. Moving water can take many forms, from the simplest single water spout to an elaborate tiered fountain. Movement brings different pleasures and can create a huge

Above: A canal of dark still water crosses the width of a lushly planted garden.

Right: Circular planters float on a pond, with an illuminated Perspex fountain creating a strong focal point.

Opposite: The smooth sheen of water slides over a glass sphere by Allison Armour-Wilson.

range of visual effects. It can be exhilarating – the sparkling water droplets of a fine spray can appear to effervesce in sunlight, and the foamy bubbles created by a jet of water hitting a still pool beneath produce turmoil on the calm surface. But movement can also be soothing: the gentle sheen of water falling in an unbroken sheet down a glass or polished metal surface is mesmerizing. The sounds that these various types of movement create can be as varied as the visual effects.

Children are particularly drawn to water, though it seems to bring out the playful side in all of us. It's a challenge to design a water feature that will be both stunning and safe for the kids. But if you do introduce a water feature – no matter how small – into a garden with small children, it is imperative that you put safety before sensation. Luckily there are some good ways to make a water garden safe

as well as attractive. Place a metal grid just below or level with the surface of the water. Choose a simple gurgling pebble pool or a smooth object with water slipping over its surface: both will fascinate children. But if you want to have more movement, make sure the water from a wall fountain or spout falls into a covered reservoir.

a water garden, *designed by* **Paul Cooper**

Left: The spectacular water cascade at Chatsworth in Derbyshire.

Opposite: Although smaller in scale, the water curtain in Henley also sparkles with movement.

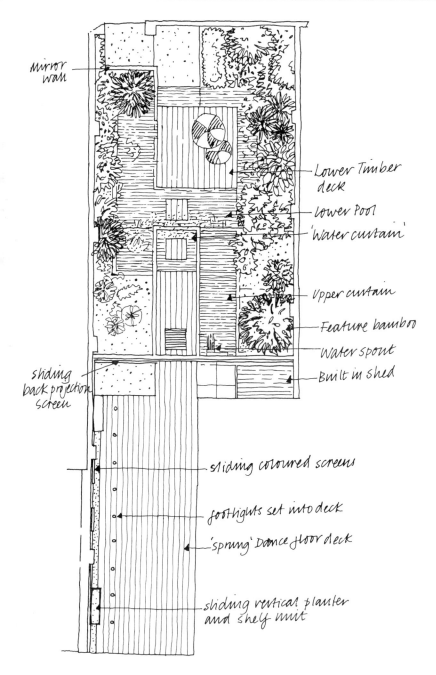

Mirror wall

Lower Timber deck

Lower Pool

'Water curtain'

Upper curtain

Feature bamboo

Water spout

Built in shed

sliding back projection screen

sliding coloured screens

footlights set into deck

'spring' Dance floor deck

sliding vertical planter and shelf unit

Sometimes the problems that affect your garden are completely beyond your control. The small town garden in picturesque Henley-on-Thames chosen for this case study was already quite pretty, if rather conventional, and contained some well-established plants. The problem lay not within the garden, but outside its boundaries. Just over the wall at the bottom of the garden there used to be an orchard. Today a vast supermarket car park, and beyond that the enormous supermarket itself, have taken the place of billowing blossom and luscious fruits. The sound of car ignitions and the beeping of juggernauts reversing to deliver their goods was constant, and with the supermarket open all hours, there was little respite from the noise.

Visually the supermarket could be thought an eyesore. But the garden owners had decided not to dwell on the negative aspects, but to try to appreciate the vitality and hustle and bustle of city life. As a bonus, a mature sycamore tree screened out much of the view, and the garden was a couple of metres higher than the level of the car park. This meant that although the garden afforded a clear view of people pushing trolleys to their cars, the people themselves were unable to see into the garden.

This plot was typical of many small gardens in Britain, tucked behind a late Victorian terraced house with no direct access from the road. At the rear, however, a narrow passageway

Left: Contrasting materials are combined to add interest and variety to a small space.

Opposite: Movable brightly coloured screens glide smoothly on wheels along a track, giving maximum flexibility.

ran along the back of all the gardens in the street. The shape of the garden was rectangular, with one corner notched out by the kitchen conversion, which protruded from the back of the house. This created a narrower strip of rather shady garden outside the kitchen door. The owners were keen to improve their plot, and had an interest in plants – though the tatty scrap of lawn suggested otherwise – but were desperately in need of inspiration. At present this was a traditional-looking garden, and rather dull for a lively young couple with plenty of interests. One of them is a keen dancer and jokingly suggested incorporating a dance area. The other was particularly keen on the attractive, low-level, red-brick walls that surrounded the garden and didn't want them hidden by climbing plants. They both agreed that something had to be done about the noise so that they could really start to enjoy their under-used garden.

It was accepted that getting rid of the source of the din was impossible and what was needed was some form of distraction. The pleasant burbling and splashing sounds of moving water would draw attention away from the traffic noise, so it seemed a good idea to try to incorporate some sort of water feature in the new garden.

This couple would be fun clients to work with; they, and the garden, needed a designer who would deal with the noise issue, loved working with water and could come up with something unusual with an extra twist. Paul Cooper (see Designers' Biographies, page 122) was without question the man for the job. A highly respected, cutting-edge designer with a string of awards to his name, Paul regularly produces ideas that no one else would think of. Strongly visual, his gardens are pure theatre. Sometimes they resemble a sculptural installation, the entire space becoming a work of art. Above all Paul's work is imbued with a sense of humour and a certain irreverence.

At the first meeting, various thoughts about how to deal with the noise problem were bandied about. Paul agreed that the use of water would be ideal as a distraction and suggested that he might introduce two or more different water sounds. It all seemed very promising and, after listening to the owners' wish list and taking measurements of the plot, Paul headed for his studio.

part of the section furthest from the house would be entirely covered with water, which would in turn be covered by metal grids, to give the impression of quite literally walking on water. Specimen plants were to be placed in gravel-covered beds between the two sections. Another smaller area of decking was positioned towards the end of the garden, surrounded by further beds packed with planting.

The details of Paul's design made it utterly unique. This was to be primarily a water garden, and Paul had succeeded in introducing the different sounds of running water he had spoken about in the initial meeting. Water was to flow from a minimal wall fountain on the back of the shed wall into the top pool. It then flowed over three narrow slabs of slate, spaced equally along the length of the wider lower pool, from where it was pumped back up to the wall fountain. But there was a trick up Paul's sleeve. A simple wooden vertical structure was to be constructed where the two sections of the garden met. At first sight this was simply a contemporary-looking pergola, something to stretch the garden up towards the sky. But at the end of the structure Paul had devised a water curtain, and when it was turned on, a sheet of water fell in fine threads of liquid to the pool below. It was a magical effect, particularly when the sunlight caught the water or when the wind blew the curtain to

Following a period of contemplation, and a visit to the remarkable water gardens at Chatsworth House for further inspiration, Paul was ready to unveil the finished design, He had produced a three-dimensional working model rather than the usual flatplan. This was wise, given the complexity of the design; the clients were expecting water, but what they got was much more than your average water feature. The garden was to be transformed: the design made the most of the vertical plane, and many unusual features would guide the eye upwards. With this much excitement crammed into a small space, who would notice a car park?

The garden was to be divided into two main sections. A properly sprung deck would create a dance floor outside the kitchen, which could also be furnished with a table and chairs to double as an eating area. A large

transport them anywhere in the world. But the biggest surprise for the unsuspecting visitor was an industrial electric fan set into the decking beneath a grille just at the point where the two sections of the garden met. The motor was to be linked to a movement sensor which switched itself on as someone walked over the grille, providing a sudden whoosh of air and possibly causing the same effect the subway vent had on Marilyn Monroe's famous white dress.

The weedy lawn was the first thing to go, but the tedious work of excavating the site was slowed by lack of proper access to the garden. It took several days to dig down to the necessary level entirely by hand, with many barrow-loads of soil to go in the skip. Once the profile of the land was correctly shaped, brick retaining walls could be built to create strong sides to the pond areas. Large sheets of butyl pond-liner were laid over a thick bed of sand to stop sharp objects from puncturing the liner. The remaining walls and red-brick pond edges were completed before any excess liner was trimmed away.

one side. Interaction between the garden and the user is an important aspect of Paul's work. Here you had a choice either to walk around the side of the curtain to avoid getting wet or to go straight through it. On a hot day the second option would be a deliciously cooling experience, and a sure-fire hit with children.

However, it was with some of the other design elements that Paul had really given his imagination full rein. Vertical sliding screens in different colours were fitted with wheels that ran along a narrow runner at the base of the wall surrounding the dance floor. These could be moved at will to produce constantly changing effects. A large white divider turned out to be a back-projection screen. This could completely block the supermarket from view while the house owners were dining outdoors, and at night images of paintings, landscapes, flowers or family holiday photos could

The sprung dance floor was installed directly on top of the existing paviours, using layers of rubber sandwiched between them and the timber decking. At the end of the garden the rest of the decking formed the square terrace, which was to be bordered on two sides by water. On the back wall of the kitchen a small

but perfectly formed shed was built. This would house garden tools and bikes, which were supported vertically by hooks in order to save space. This was also the place for the switches and controls for the water pumps and the electric fan. A low-level wall continued from the back of the shed – which was painted a fresh, clear turquoise – on to which a beautifully sleek water spout was fixed.

The vertical structure in the centre of the garden was constructed entirely from exterior-grade marine ply to ensure longevity, and the pipes to carry the water to the water curtain were run up to the top along grooves in the timbers. The curtain 'rail' was simply a length of plastic pipe, drilled at regular intervals along its length, which was then fixed to the horizontal beam at the end of the structure.

Pumps were installed in each pond to circulate the water, one in the higher pond and three in the lower – including one to pump the water up to the curtain. It was crucial to the success of the garden that the pumps were correctly balanced. At one stage the water pressure was too great in the top pool, causing water to gush over the slates – which were fixed at three points at the edge of the top pool – into the lower pond. But with a bit of fine-tuning, the correct levels were achieved and it was time to move on.

With all the workings of the water garden in place, the metal grids could be lowered on to the ponds. These were made from galvanized steel and were incredibly heavy. It took several men to cut them to shape, spray the cut ends with protective anti-rust galvanizing spray and lay them slowly in place. But before they could go down, there was an important job to do.

Paul wanted to bring in something living to soften the hard lines of the grilles and had chosen a couple of aquatic plants. *Iris versicolor* 'Kermesina' is an American water iris with stunning deep purple flowers in June or July and slender, strap-like leaves. As a contrast, *Schoenoplectus lacustris* subsp. *tabernaemontani* 'Zebrinus' has spiky leaves, striped like a zebra, as well as an unpronounceable name. They were both planted in plastic baskets, which were filled with aquatic compost, topped up with a thick layer of gravel and gently lowered into the pond.

The complex landscaping and mechanics of Paul's design were complete; it was time to get the plants in. A magnificent bamboo, *Phyllostachys nigra*, was given pride of place next to the wall fountain, its foliage contrasting wonderfully with the blue wall. To set it off perfectly, a layer of pale gravel was raked around its base. Three large *Elaeagnus × ebbingei* were planted by the end wall to

provide a dense protective shield from the noise beyond. A ghostly *Rubus thibetanus* 'Silver Fern' was also positioned at the end of the garden, this time directly in front of an acrylic mirror. This had the effect of beefing up the number of white-bloomed stems and gave the illusion that the planting area had doubled in size. The leaves of *Berberis × media* 'Red Jewel' toned perfectly with the brick walls, and the pure white, cheery flowers of *Anemone × hybrida* 'Honorine Jobert' danced above a group of thymes that Paul had planted beneath another metal grid. They would soon fill out to cover the walkway with a carpet of fragrant foliage.

Paul encouraged the owners to put their own stamp on the garden immediately. The movable screens around the dance floor needed painting and Paul insisted they choose the colours themselves. The results were just as he had hoped – modern, slightly off-the-wall tones, so to speak, that justified his faith in their good taste. A couple of large square terracotta containers had been purchased to dress the gravel area between the dance floor and the water. Again, on Paul's suggestion, the owners were to choose the planting combination. Once more, the result was a brilliant success: the reddish leaves of *Panicum virgatum* 'Squaw' and the maroon-toned, squirrel-tailed flowers of *Pennisetum alopecuroïdes* 'Hameln' mingled with *Sedum* 'Ruby Glow', which spilled over the edge in the most ravishing, slightly dishevelled fashion.

As a final touch Paul created a vertical vegetable garden on another movable screen near the dance floor. Young seedlings could be nurtured beneath a protective Perspex cover, and a row of herbs was ready for picking just by the kitchen door.

One of the main advantages of having a small garden is that the total effect of a scheme is not diluted, as it often can be when lost within a large space. Paul's cutting-edge design for this small town garden is totally uncompromising in its clarity of vision. It reflects his own sense of humour and the open minds of the owners, and is absolutely crammed with originality. Everyone agreed that this was more than a garden: it was a total sensory experience.

Left: The sound of moving water can be gently soothing.

Opposite: A greater volume of water will screen out unwanted noise as it splashes on to a still pool.

noise *and* pollution

As the owners of the garden in Henley soon discovered, noise pollution is a major problem for city dwellers; creating your own urban paradise is hard when you can't hear yourself think. The constant drone of traffic is something you become so accustomed to that when you are somewhere really quiet, the silence is almost tangible. Other familiar urban noises – the din of building sites, circling police helicopters, pubs emptying at night, reversing lorries and screeching motorbike couriers – impinge even on the background growling of the cars. Those of us who live in towns need to find some respite from the unrelenting cacophony of sounds. The garden is the perfect place to bring some serenity back into your life, but to do that it's imperative to try to create a calm, if not quiet, atmosphere.

Planting a living barrier to act as a buffer against undesirable noise is sometimes advised, and a screening of densely foliaged hedges or shrubs is often suggested. It's questionable whether plants have any measurable physical effect in noise reduction, and unlikely that they can actually 'absorb' it. But they give the psychological impression of doing just that. Perhaps the feeling of separateness and protection that a screen of greenery gives helps to foster the illusion that the sound is deadened.

It's generally a far better plan to use distraction: create your own pleasing sounds within the garden and the exterior noise won't be so obvious. Water is perfect for this – the soothing effect of a gently flowing wall fountain can transport you to a citrus-filled, Mediterranean courtyard; the sparkling sound of water cascading from a spout into a pool below may remind you of the surf; and the bubbling of a pebble fountain conjures up images of a rural brook. Unfortunately, many water features are more reminiscent of a flushing lavatory or an irritating running tap, thereby adding to the unwanted sounds. Some adjustment to the water outlet or the rate of flow is usually all that's needed to resolve the problem.

City noise can add to the stress of urban life, but there is another form of pollution that affects town dwellers in particular: atmospheric pollution, from traffic fumes and industrial activity, is ultimately a far more sinister threat. Trees provide a vital lifeline for towns, and Britain's cities are thankfully far greener than many equivalents abroad, but things could still be improved. Our urban trees are such a vital resource that many are safeguarded by protection orders. However, those that are not are frequently cut down without any plan to plant a replacement and in this way the number of trees is gradually depleted. I feel that if you can incorporate a tree in your garden – and many are suitable for even very small gardens – you almost have a duty to do so. This is simply forward-

thinking good sense. Trees absorb carbon dioxide and produce oxygen – they are the lungs of a city and therefore future generations depend on us to keep planting young saplings now.

Some plants can suffer quite badly from the effects of pollution, but luckily there are others that will thrive in the heart of the big smoke. The London plane often springs to mind when city trees are mentioned, but of course it's far too large for most domestic gardens and is primarily a street tree. The hawthorn family is pollution-tolerant, and *Crataegus laevigata* 'Paul's Scarlet', with its clusters of rosy-red flowers, is a good choice for a small space. Alternatively, members of the prunus, pyrus and malus families are also excellent contenders for gardens on busy main roads. Hollies are tough plants for this situation, and *Ilex × altaclerensis* 'Belgica

Aurea' has a compact, columnar shape with cream edges to the glossy green leaves and plenty of scarlet berries in the autumn.

For something a little smaller, try a lilac: *Syringa vulgaris* 'Madame Lemoine' is a popular variety, with plumes of headily scented, white flowers towards the end of tspring. Buddleias are also pollution-tolerant and will attract butterflies into your garden. Smaller still are the evergreen skimmias. *Skimmia × confusa* 'Kew Green' has fragrant white flowers atop its dark green leaves. Other good evergreens include members of the elaeagnus, euonymus and sarcococca families. If it's perennials you're after, there is a wide selection to choose from. One of my favourites is *Astrantia major* 'Hadspen Blood', with diminutive but devastatingly attractive plummy-red flowers. As a bonus it will also cope with the semi-shade conditions found in many town gardens.

using
the
vertical

Small gardens can be incredibly restrictive in terms of useful space. A regular trick of top designers is to extend the garden by using the vertical dimension: the area above ground level is so often completely forgotten. It helps to think of your garden in three-dimensional terms – not as a flat piece of ground, but as a space that includes the air above it. If you can't spread out, you can at least go up.

On a practical note, it's wise to check the local planning regulations on erecting structures in the garden. You probably won't need planning permission, but there may be restrictions relating to the height of walls and other structural elements. In any case, it is simply good manners to show a certain amount of neighbourly awareness when constructing anything that may affect those around you.

Paul Cooper found myriad ways of using the vertical space in the Henley garden. You may prefer to use just one, but this is still preferable to restricting the design of the garden to the horizontal plane. One of the most traditional ways of adding height is with a pergola, usually a simple timber structure consisting of upright and crossing beams. This can be updated, as it was in Henley, by a very slight alteration to the design. Rose arches and tripods are also ways to incorporate vertical wooden features. These are all wonderful supports for climbers, if it is your aim to make the most of the airspace for growing plants, and are often attractive design elements in their unadorned state.

Stone columns add stature to a garden and work well in a formal space, but there's no reason (other than the restriction of cost) that these couldn't be made of Perspex or galvanized sheet steel. Updating a classic feature in this way gives you all the benefits of a style that has lasted thousands of years, with a modern twist. Other metals can also be crafted into beautiful structures. Copper, which is best treated with varnish or lacquer, can be fashioned into an obelisk to create height in the middle of a border or stand alone as a feature sculpture. Water features can also be used to extend the space vertically. Wall-spouts, water sculptures and fountains can all add interest at eye level. Tall containers of varying heights can be constructed to stand in a shallow pond and be filled with planting.

Varying the planting levels is one of the best ways to liven up a garden. Raised beds are the simplest way to achieve this, but the effect will be more interesting if you can introduce several different heights and shapes of bed, juxtaposed one against the other. Build up one section of the garden in this way and you will avoid the uniformity that often goes with borders at ground level backed by a wall or fence. You can also create outdoor shelving systems to hold an assortment of containers.

Fill small pots with a collection of alpines so that you can enjoy their ravishing flowers at close quarters without having to bend down. Alternatively, use larger pots and cram them with cheerful annuals for a full-on blast of colour. Place trailing plants on the higher shelves and allow them to cascade down the side. This type of tiered planting is particularly good for edible plants when positioned outside the kitchen door. Use it for growing herbs and small salad crops, such as rocket. Pop the dwarf tomato 'Tumbler' into a pot at the top of the stack where the fruits can hang over the edge.

Climbing plants are perfect for guiding the eye upwards. In a small space you may want to avoid anything too vigorous. *Solanum jasminoïdes* 'Album' is a beautiful plant, smothered in starry white flowers at the end of summer. But if you don't want your climber to reach more than 6m (20ft) up the back wall of the house, it's best avoided. With such a wide range of climbing plants, there is something for every eventuality. There are many good climbers for shade: a huge diversity of ivies, the stalwart self-clinging *Hydrangea anomala* subsp. *petiolaris*, *Clematis* 'Nelly Moser', which retains the dusky pink of its saucer-shaped blooms far better in the shade, and *Rosa* 'Madame Alfred Carrière', with its softly shaped white flowers. *Euonymous* 'Silver Queen' is best known as a good, low-growing, evergreen filler, but this variegated beauty – tolerant of sun or shade – will also snake its way up a conveniently placed wall to form a compact covering of foliage.

There are so many good climbers for sunny walls that it will be hard to make your choice. Most roses and wisterias prefer a position in full sun, and also partial to basking in the heat is the honeysuckle *Lonicera periclymenum* 'Graham Thomas', which releases the full intensity of its sweet scent on summer evenings. Clematis push their heads up into the light, but prefer some cool shade at their feet. *Passiflora caerulea*, the passion flower, is currently a fashionable plant and its exotic looks are perfect for a garden with a tropical feel. Wall shrubs make good vertical interest plants; *Ceanothus griseus* var. *horizontalis* 'Yankee Point' is a compact variety, which will fan itself out against a low wall if given a few judicious nips and tucks.

Above left: With a purpose-built compost bin, mini greenhouse and cloche, functional items can become a pleasure to look at.

Above right: Vegetables are not only tasty but beautiful too.

Opposite left: A reclaimed brick barbecue provides a permanent outdoor cooking area.

Opposite right: The dusky bloom of black grapes.

the **edible garden**

Nowadays we are all increasingly aware of the importance of knowing where what we eat comes from. Living in a city is no barrier to growing your own edible plants. The trick in a small space is knowing how to combine the practical with the visual, to create a garden that provides tasty produce and a beautiful space in which to relax. It's so rewarding to eat what you have grown yourself and picked only moments before. Once you've experienced the freshness and flavour of home-grown fruit and vegetables, there's no turning back.

What could be nicer than stepping out of your back door and harvesting a lettuce still dripping with dew from your own garden? A quick rinse and the leaves are ready to eat, fresh, crisp and sweet. This might seem like a dream to town gardeners, but historically city dwellers devoted whatever meagre space they had outside their houses entirely to growing edible plants; only the very rich could afford to waste space on ornamental plants. Today we are turning once again to making our gardens productive as well as beautiful, and there are many ways to make the most of a limited space.

One option is to incorporate edibles throughout, designing a flower garden specifically to include fruit and vegetables among the ornamental plants. Alternatively, try a twist on the traditional potager; this name for an ornamental vegetable garden is derived from the French word *potage*, meaning 'soup'. As well as providing the ingredients for a soup, these kitchen gardens resembled one, the mixture of different vegetables, salads and fruits all jostling for space in one place. Potagers were often laid out on formal lines, with small box hedges marking the divisions between the beds. This created individual planting compartments to be filled with a vast range of vegetables and herbs. The result was both practical and decorative, the colourful mix of varieties and symmetry of the designs making them very easy on the eye.

Even if the garden is primarily an ornamental one, edible plants can still be grown very successfully among the shrubs and perennials. Plant parsley as an edging to a flower bed, and include ruby chard in a 'hot' planting scheme for its stunning blood-red stems. The feathery

Left: A herb border containing artemisia, mentha, *Anthriscus cerefolium*, lovage and a selection of thymus makes a decorative and aromatic edging.

Opposite: A variety of galvanized metal pots containing herbs and ornamentals are within easy reach of the kitchen.

For a movable feast, plant salads, vegetables and herbs in containers. Choose pots that suit the style of the garden – galvanized metal for sleek modern spaces, terracotta or timber Versailles planters in more traditional plots. Don't forget the space above ground level: some varieties of dwarf tomato are particularly well suited to growing in hanging baskets, provided they're not allowed to dry out. Higher still, why not grow vegetables on roof gardens: use large planters, keep them well watered by installing a simple irrigation system and they'll thrive in the good light. Window-boxes make excellent mini vegetable plots: plant fast-growing rocket or 'Little Gem' lettuces, or pack the box with a selection of herbs for easy access outside a kitchen window. Strawberries – particularly little wild strawberries – are a perfect fruit for small areas and look lovely all year round. They can be grown in special terracotta towers, in purpose-made self-assembly stacking pots, or individually dotted around ornamental plants.

The best thing about incorporating edibles in a small garden is their flexibility. If you fancy a complete change next year, grow a different range of vegetables or salads, which will also help to avoid the build-up of soil-borne diseases. Get the bones of the garden right with structural evergreen planting to hold the design together and then play with the vast range of varieties available. Above all, enjoy the delicious results!

foliage of bronze-leaved fennel looks wonderful grown with herbaceous perennials and grasses, and the glaucous blue of certain types of cabbage is a rare and highly prized leaf colour in any plant. Fan-trained fruit trees can clothe a wall as attractively as any climber, smothered with blossom in spring and heavy with fruit by the autumn.

an edible garden *designed by* **Bunny Guinness**

Left: A corner of the potager at the Old Rectory in Sudborough, Bunny's inspiration for the edible small garden.

Opposite: Strategically placed willow arches backed with mirror panels hint at areas of garden beyond, waiting to be explored.

At first sight this garden in St Albans in Hertfordshire seemed to have very little going for it. It formed an awkward L-shape tacked on as an afterthought to a newly built house. Like many recent building projects, the house was squeezed on to a plot that had once been part of someone else's back garden. There was a steeply raised area banked up along one side of the property, creating an uncomfortably narrow passageway against the wall of the house. This side of the garden was dominated by a row of semi-mature leylandii trees backing on to wooded common land. The result was a dark, useless space with a few rather forlorn-looking shrubs dotted about. The other arm of the L-shape formed the main part of the garden and was accessed from the house by patio doors. This area linked with the passageway and was covered for the most part in crazy paving, with some shrubs and a couple of large conifers tucked into the edges of the garden.

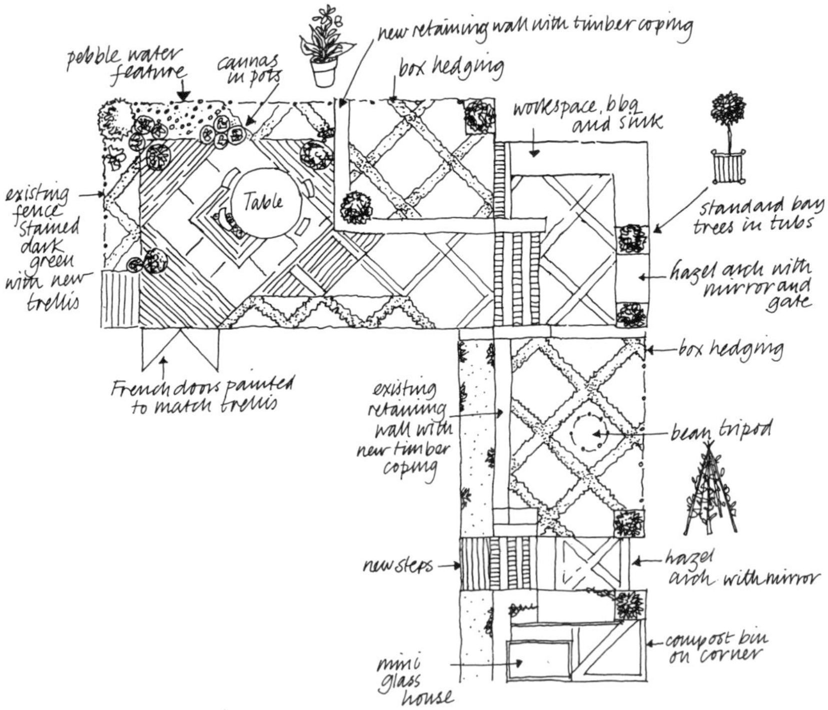

The neighbouring buildings and gardens created additional problems: a tall blue pergola on the other side of the fence was clearly visible, and there was the potential problem of being overlooked if too many of the taller plants were removed. The owners are keen cooks and the tatty old barbecue had seen plenty of action. The brief here was to create a garden that brought this love of food and cookery to the fore by making the space productive in terms of vegetables and herbs. In addition, it had to be an attractive, child-friendly space for entertaining friends and family, with room to indulge the barbecue bug and party well into the night.

This was a demanding brief for any designer. It needed someone who could come up with a visually attractive solution for this awkward plot, while having a real understanding of the practical aspects of growing edible plants and the needs of children and a sociable couple who love to cook. Enter Bunny Guinness (see Designers' Biographies, page 122), who, as a five-times gold medal-winning designer at the Chelsea Flower Show, mother of two, keen cook and all-round super-gardener, was just the person for the job.

Garden plan labels:

pebble water feature

cannas in pots

new retaining wall with timber coping

box hedging

workspace, bbq and sink

existing fence stained dark green with new trellis

Table

standard bay trees in tubs

hazel arch with mirror and gate

French doors painted to match trellis

existing retaining wall with new timber coping

box hedging

bean tripod

new steps

hazel arch with mirror

compost bin on corner

mini glass house

Left: Changes of level draw the eye to the built-in outdoor kitchen area.

Opposite left: Carved pineapple finials provide the finishing touch.

Opposite below: Wavy trellis topped with woven willow is a novel twist on a conventional design.

Bunny had several meetings with the owners, discussing their particular requirements, and getting to know their likes and dislikes. The garden was carefully measured and photographed, and Bunny went off to let it all sink in before commencing work on the design. What she came up with is an incredibly imaginative use of a difficult space. The design, a contemporary take on the traditional potager, addresses all the problems and has found effective solutions. Bunny combined ornamental plants with edibles, reshaped existing trees and gave the whole garden structure a framework of diagonal lines in the form of paving detail and low box hedging criss-crossing the small space.

The first step was to clear the garden. The leylandii trees were the first to go. Once they were down, the small plot immediately opened up, metres of space were gained and light flooded in. One is often reluctant to make such drastic changes to a garden, not least because it involves killing plants. But being ruthless is often the only way to bring out the true potential of a space; sometimes you just have to take a deep breath and do it. One of the two large conifers was also removed, but the other, in the opposite corner of the garden, was transformed from a conical shape into a standard by having all its lower branches stripped away. This was a clever way of retaining the height of the tree, to provide screening from the neighbours' upper windows, while clearing the space beneath the newly formed crown. The result was a more formally shaped tree that fitted in perfectly with the style of the new garden.

Clearing can be extremely therapeutic, and lifting the crazy paving, which came up easily, was a cathartic experience. Landscaping the plot followed. The top of the raised area to the side of the house was levelled and steps cut into it to give the appearance of widening the restrictive passageway and to allow access on to the raised space. To the rear of the house a large, mid-height raised bed was created, butting up to the existing raised section in the corner of the L-shape. In this way a series of interesting changes of level was developed, making maximum use of the available space.

Plenty of thought went into the choice of landscaping materials. Large, square stone paving slabs were laid diagonally across the garden, divided by narrow rows of stone setts. These lines of setts were picked up exactly in the lines formed by the tiny box plants that would soon grow together to form solid dividing hedges. A coping of wood was added, raising the height of the existing retaining walls of the raised area and creating a useful place to sit. Panels of unusual trellis, constructed with wavy strips of wood and painted Bunny's favourite shade of blue, quickly went up around the boundary.

Above right: Among the edibles, companion planting of marigolds will attract beneficial insects that help to control unwanted pests.

Although at first sight this is a garden rooted in traditional style, much of the detail is thoroughly modern.

But the *pièce de résistance* was the outdoor kitchen, designed for serious entertaining and constructed by a master craftsman in a deceptively simple, rusticated style from blocks of heavy oak; the worktops were solid enough to last a lifetime. A state-of-the-art gas barbecue hob was concealed until needed under a lift-up worktop. Set into the unit was a chunky drawer for storing cooking implements, and a deep sink for rinsing off freshly harvested salad leaves. Bunny dressed the area with terracotta pots containing herbs, to be picked as needed during cooking.

Bunny's eye for detail is second to none, and the decorative touches she introduced made the garden instantly recognizable as a 'Bunny Guinness garden'. Finials in the shape of pineapples were added to the tops of the posts

connecting the trellis panels and were repeated on the corners of the Versailles planters. They were originally designed to be painted gold, replicating gilding with gold leaf, but Bunny decided after experimenting with one finial that she preferred them in their natural state. A lion's-head mask that acted as a spout for the wall-fountain was gilded and glowed triumphantly through a wreath of ivy. The water falls from the mask on to a small basin at ground level, lined with plaster casts of fossil ammonites. The ammonite detail is picked up in other parts of the garden, with some embedded into the soil around the base of one of the standard bay trees, the gaps filled with gravel to act as a decorative mulch.

To create the illusion of extra space beyond the boundary, Bunny placed woven willow arches at two strategic points on the raised side of the garden. The first, directly opposite the kitchen door, invites you to step up to the little terraced area; the other, near the outdoor kitchen, elongates the sight line across the widest part of the garden. The backs of the arches were filled in with mirror panels, accentuating the illusion of infinite space beyond. Although at first sight this is a garden rooted in traditional style, much of the detail is thoroughly modern. The sides of the Versailles planters are made of galvanized metal, and the wavy trellis gives a modern twist to a classic design. This individual

combination of traditional and contemporary style is what makes the garden so successful and utterly unique.

With the landscaping finished, the garden had become a blank sculptural canvas and planting could commence, bringing Bunny's design to life. First to go in was the structural backbone planting. The crossing rows of small box plants were planted 20 cm (8 in) apart and the tops were trimmed immediately to encourage them to bush out from the base. *Buxus sempervirens* was chosen, which is faster-growing and less susceptible to disease than the dwarf form, *Buxus sempervirens* 'Suffruticosa'. Several standard clipped bays were placed strategically around the garden, with one taking pride of place on the front corner of the new raised bed, creating a visual full stop.

Finally, the sections could be filled in with vegetables. We planted late in the season, so used small, ready-grown, individual plants; an increasingly wide selection is available as plug plants from garden centres in the spring. But for a better range of varieties, and to cut costs considerably, the owners plan to raise the majority themselves from seed next year. To facilitate this and to give protection to tender vegetables, such as aubergines and peppers, Bunny designed an ingenious mini-greenhouse to stand against the wall at the end of the garden, next to an equally

attractive compost bin. In a small space everything in it is on show, so it should be beautiful as well as functional. The ingenuity of the greenhouse design is in its flexibility: large doors open by folding into smaller sections, which prevents them from blocking the passageway to the back gate, and the lid can be raised to increase ventilation when necessary in hot weather.

In the bed to the side of the house a tower of French beans gave height to the central area. Each surrounding compartment created by the box divisions was planted with a different vegetable or salad crop. Since this potager constitutes the entire garden, the varieties were chosen for their decorative qualities, as well as for taste, and were arranged to be pleasing to the eye. The blood-red stems of a ruby chard contrasted with the glaucous bluish-green of brassica foliage. Contrast was also to be found in the variation of heights, texture and leaf shapes, with curly-leaved parsley next to purple sage and baby leeks. In the future it will be wise for the owners to rotate the plants in each section, just as you would in a conventional vegetable garden, to prevent the build-up of disease-causing organisms in the soil.

To prevent gaps forming once a crop had been harvested, Bunny suggested the use of cut-and-come-again salads, where you remove from the lettuce only what you need for that

meal, leaving the main plant *in situ* to grow on. In compartments that had been cleared completely, ornamental bedding could be introduced: French marigolds look jolly, and their strong scent is a great deterrent to unwanted pests and an attractant to beneficial insects, so using them as companion planting is both decorative and useful. In the winter, when the range of vegetables grown would be greatly depleted, winter-flowering pansies and violas would add colour and happily take the place of the harvested vegetables. Colour and interest in the beds needn't be confined to the plants: terracotta rhubarb forcers and glazed mini-cloches were introduced for practical and decorative purposes.

Ornamental plants were also added to the borders surrounding the paved area. Towering cannas planted around the wall-fountain brought a touch of the exotic to the garden, and clouds of pink-flowered cosmos would go on blooming for months above frothy green foliage. Ivy was introduced beneath the large conifer, where a tough plant was needed to survive the dry shade. More ivy was added to climb through the trellis around the lion's-head mask, where it would soften the edges in no time at all. Other climbers were incorporated, including a pre-existing fruiting grapevine and the evergreen *Clematis armandii*, which would be smothered with scented white flowers in early spring and thrive in the semi-shady conditions found in parts of the garden.

The beauty of the planting in this garden lies in its great flexibility. Within the long-term framework of box hedging the plants can be changed year by year to include any combination of edible and ornamental plants. Should the owners decide to have a complete change, the garden could easily be completely turned over to flowering plants, using annuals within the compartments, or perennials if a more permanent scheme is preferred. The colour theme can also be changed on a whim – one year hot, spicy shades can predominate, the next icy cool white and blue, altering entirely the atmosphere of the space.

In practical terms the garden fulfils the brief exactly. I joined the party the first time that guests were invited and the garden looked beautiful and functioned perfectly on every level. Entertaining was easy-going and comfortable, with people perched informally on the walls and steps, as well as using the seating area. Plates overflowed with freshly picked corn-on-the-cob dripping with butter and sizzling meat barbecued with home-grown herbs. Candles flickered and glasses of wine were passed back and forth in a space that felt far from cramped. The garden was filled with the scent of aromatic plants, children traced the shape of the fossils in the pool of water and happy laughter filled the air. From the most unpromising of plots has emerged a beautiful garden that really works.

Left: Introduce a touch of
the Mediterranean with a
fruiting vine.

Opposite: The perfect
setting for dining al fresco
amid lush planting.

entertaining
in the
garden

One of the greatest pleasures of having a
garden is being able to share it with others,
and Bunny Guinness's scheme certainly
enhanced that pleasure. Enjoyable memories
of endless summer evenings spent with
family and friends can sustain us through a
long hard winter, and with the advent of
effective outdoor heaters there's no reason
not to be able to party all night on New Year's
Eve. Socializing outside makes the experience
far more relaxed and informal, and of course
it's the perfect opportunity to show off all the
hard work you've done in the garden and talk
plants with other keen gardeners.

Cooking outdoors instantly turns into
something more exciting than just
providing a meal. Keen barbecue cooks treat
the whole experience as a performance,
with much heated discussion about recipes
for marinades, optimum cooking
temperatures and the virtues of charcoal
versus gas barbecues. In view of the pleasure
gained from entertaining in the garden, it
makes sense to consider all the
practicalities when planning the layout,
particularly in a small garden where space is
always at a premium.

You need to consider how much cooking
you like to do, whether you are happy to buy
the occasional disposable barbecue, or if you
want a state-of-the-art outdoor kitchen.
Whatever your requirements, choose

something that will fit in with the overall
style of the garden – plenty of sleek metal in
a modern garden, and a recycled brick
barbecue in a traditional plot. In small
town gardens the usual advice to position
the cooking area near the kitchen door is
irrelevant as every part of the garden will be
close enough. So you can be led by other
design considerations and select the
spot where it will look most pleasing, or be
least obtrusive, depending on your
preference.

Seating is equally important; guests will feel
much more comfortable if there is
somewhere to sit down. If you have an area of
lawn, this will never be a problem as rugs and
cushions can be scattered where needed and
food can be served picnic-style. In gardens
with a hard landscaped floor, incorporate
perching places in the design – the edges of
raised beds, pools and steps are all perfect for
informal chatting. Furniture becomes vital,
however, when you want to provide a sit-
down meal, and where you position the
dining area will have some bearing on the
atmosphere that is created. Placing a table
beneath the lower branches of a mature tree
will provide a hint of rural life and dappled
shade from midday sun. Tucking the table
next to a boundary, rather than right in the
middle of the garden, may help to avoid a
sense of exposure. It's hard to relax while
being watched by the neighbours.

Create something so attractive that to hide it with climbers is almost a sin.

For city gardeners the main preoccupation is dealing with the neighbours. Providing a sense of privacy can be difficult when flats and houses are packed together, but gardens should help us to feel separate from the bustle of life going on around us. Creating an oasis of calm amid the turmoil isn't easy, and trying to block out the world around you completely is a mistake. Better to accept that you will probably be able to see and be seen by other residents to some extent, and improve those areas within your own domain that you can change. Boundaries are often subject to local by-laws and regulations, and these need to be checked before deciding on the height. It's tempting to make them as high as possible, but that can result in a space that feels dark and claustrophobic. If your plot has an attractive view or local feature – and many town gardens do – find a way to include it; you could consider incorporating 'windows' in the wall or fence to frame the view.

boundaries *and* screens

In small town gardens we are all too aware of what surrounds us at close quarters; the boundaries are always there to remind us of the limits of our domain. Walls and fences are often neglected, and in a large garden with banks of mature shrubs you can get away with that, but in a small plot they are so visible that the best plan is to turn them into a feature.

There are many options available to us when choosing a boundary, and the range is increasing all the time. If you have old brick walls, try to keep them, unless they really don't work with a sleek, modern design. You can always raise walls that are too low by adding trellis or woven willow panels. Boring brick can be rendered to give a smooth or

textured finish and painted in blocks of bright colour. Fencing, trellis and other wooden boundaries come in myriad styles and are perfect if you want to grow twining climbers, such as ivy or clematis. Living boundaries are often neglected in town gardens, with rows of dull privet giving hedges a bad name, but a careful choice of plant makes a hedge a really attractive option in the right place.

Living willow and bamboo screens can be planted along a conventional fence to soften the hard edges, or form a living space divider. Dividing up the plot is a technique used in large gardens all the time, but it's just as effective in a small space, giving the illusion that there is much more to the garden than meets the eye. The best dividers form screens that allow glimpses of what lies beyond, rather than solid barriers. For a traditional effect, that old favourite, wrought iron, can

look particularly attractive, especially when it supports climbing roses, clematis or honeysuckle. In modern spaces low walls of glass bricks are really effective, particularly when used in conjunction with imaginative lighting effects at night.

Mirrors can also help give the illusion of added space. A little goes a long way, but when positioned behind a feature plant they can double the effect it creates. By reflecting light they can lift dark corners and, when strategically placed in false doorways and arches, extend the garden into the land of make-believe. Walls covered in sheets of galvanized metal and beaten copper and zinc are still at the cutting edge of boundary design. These shiny reflective (but not mirrored) surfaces are perfect for a state-of-the-art minimalist garden and would be particularly effective in an enclosed shady courtyard.

Above left: The graceful fronds of *Stipa gigantea* are silhouetted against the chimney pots.

Above right: A subdued palette of colours works perfectly in this traditionally styled terrace garden.

Opposite left: Make the most of every available space to bring greenery into your environment.

Opposite middle: Tall, galvanized metal containers are filled with sun-loving plants.

Opposite right: Timber decking is the perfect flooring for rooftop gardens.

the **roof garden**

There is a garden for every location and the most inhospitable of conditions. Roof-top and balcony gardens present a range of problems to overcome, not least exposure to the elements and lack of privacy. But it is possible to create something special in the most unpromising places and the result can be a unique, high-rise, inner-city paradise. There is a perverse pleasure in solving design problems, so look for the potential, be imaginative and create an oasis among the rooftops.

Left: Design details are all-important in a small garden.

Opposite: An oasis of calm nestles among the urban rooftops.

Such is our love of plants and gardens that we strive to create outdoor space wherever we can. If you've nowhere to garden at ground level but have a bit of flat roof, you can go up in the world. Properly constructed roof gardens add value to your property and are now a common sight in our cities, where the rooftop landscape is often punctuated by hints of foliage and flashes of colour. Budget permitting, even water features can be introduced. In design terms, the sky's the limit.

Gardening under an open sky is exciting, and roof-garden design has come on in leaps and bounds; an eclectic collection of mismatched pots on a bitumen surface is no longer acceptable. The design can encompass any of the style elements found in ground-level gardens, from the soft, traditional and flower-filled, to oriental Zen-like calm, to sleek and slinky modernity. If the roof terrace connects directly to one of the rooms in the house or flat, consider linking the two in terms of style; this will give a sense of continuity and spaciousness.

Many city dwellers have access not to a terrace or flat roof, but to a balcony. Tower blocks constructed in the sixties and seventies are now becoming fashionable and sought-after properties; it's time to update and make the best use of their balconies, some of which can be quite large. With a thoughtful choice of accessories, the balcony can become a really useful extension of the flat. The plants will have to be chosen carefully as high winds can howl around the top floors of tall blocks. There are several practicalities to address before you bring a single plant on to the roof. Paving and soil-filled planters are heavy, so it's vital you get a structural engineer to check the strength of the roof itself and the loading it will bear. Also, give some thought to the watering: it can be a chore to have to water a large number of containers up to twice daily in hot weather: small pots in particular dry out rapidly in high summer. Far better to think ahead at the outset and install an automatic watering system. This can be linked to a timer to continue the watering when you're not around.

Problems of exposure can take two forms. The first is the literal sense: plants can be buffeted by the elements, and without protection from sun, wind and rain, only the toughest survive. But over-exposure can also refer to the sense of openness and vulnerability you feel if overlooked by all and sundry. On high roof gardens this won't be a problem – you can simply enjoy the view below. But many city roofs will be lower than neighbouring flats and office blocks, and it's hard to relax and enjoy the garden when you feel you're being watched. If you are overlooked by taller neighbouring buildings, consider erecting some sort of screening.

Left: Sleek modern design fits perfectly with the geometric shapes of the inner-city landscape.

Opposite: Using a different approach, an abundance of flowers and verdant foliage softens the view of high-rise towers.

The hard landscaping is a backdrop to the planting, and plants on roofs need containers. Using really large planters provides one of the most effective planting solutions and creates a similar effect to planting in beds on the ground. In this way plants can be grouped in swathes, with drifts of contrasting leaf and flower colour, texture and shape flowing into one another. If you do choose individual containers, you can group collections of unmatched small pots together, creating an informal, eclectic effect. Alternatively, substantially sized containers can provide strong sculptural shapes, and the increased amount of compost they hold means you can grow a wide range of large plants. Use three or more identical pots together for the strongest design statement.

In the relative shelter of the town most plants thrive in roof gardens, but in cooler parts of the country more exposed roofs can suffer from high winds and exposure, so your choice of plants should take that into account. In cooler areas it's wise to position a row of really tough, wind-resistant plants around the roof edge. This should take the worst bite out of the weather and help to shelter less rugged plants, which can then be placed within this protective barrier.

Trellis is ideal because it allows wind to pass through it. Trying to block out anything stronger than a slight breeze with a physical barrier could be dangerous unless the barrier is extremely firmly fixed. Panels of strengthened frosted glass or Perspex would make an effective contemporary screen. Whatever you choose to surround the edge of the roof, make sure it's high enough to provide a safe barrier.

A wide range of different floorings can be suitable for roof gardens. Paving slabs look great, but may be too heavy for some roofs. Timber decking, ranging from the simplest strip flooring to highly decorative patterns, is an excellent choice. Some of the newest plastic and rubber surfaces are both lightweight and practical. Combining two or more materials is particularly effective, but avoid an over-complicated pattern.

a roof garden *designed by* **Douglas Coltart**

Left: The dramatic setting of Ian Hamilton Finlay's garden, Little Sparta, is an inspiration for Douglas Coltart.

Opposite: A rill of water follows the edge of the decking, which is punctuated by up-lighters and softened with the red-tinged foliage of *Sorbus reducta*.

When the potential of a new garden is under assessment, some sites sound more promising than others. Freezing temperatures, howling winds and total lack of protection from the rain, closely followed by periods of full, glaring sun, didn't sound great. But when you added the words 'building site', it seemed downright depressing. Yes, this roof terrace in Paisley on the outskirts of Glasgow had its fair share of problems. Complete exposure to the extreme weather conditions, a building site for a new housing development right on its doorstep, which would mean new neighbours

with a full view of the terrace, and all directly under the flight path from Glasgow airport. Why, you may ask, would anyone want to build a roof garden here?

But it wasn't all doom and gloom. The terrace was on the second floor of an attractive Victorian listed building constructed of local grey stone. A reminder of the textile industry in the Paisley area at the time, this had been the wages office, where hundreds of workers collected their pay at the end of a hard week. The building had recently been renovated and

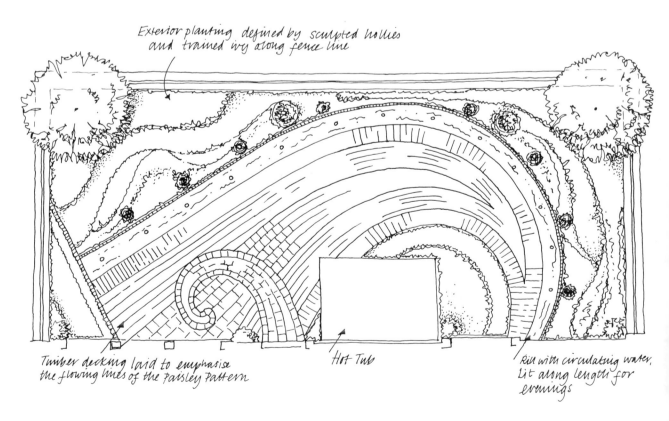

Exterior planting defined by sculpted hollies and trained ivy along fence line

Timber decking laid to emphasise the flowing lines of the Paisley Pattern

Hot Tub

Rill with circulating water, lit along length for evenings

the owners of the bleak roof terrace had created a lovely flat. A canal, on which a pair of swans drifted, followed by their adolescent cygnets, flowed gently alongside the property.

The terrace itself was a generous size, a perfect rectangle with simple railings edging the roof. An attempt had been made to do something with the space. A motley collection of pots contained some severely wind-burnt conifers, struggling to survive in bone-dry compost. The owners were eager to get maximum use from their terrace. A sociable couple with a grown-up daughter, they were particularly keen on using the outside space for entertaining. However, their previous attempts had been hampered by the weather. On one occasion a glass-topped metal table was blown off the roof and flew into the canal; had it landed a few metres further away, the consequences could have been lethal. Smaller items, such as paddling pools,

were always being whisked away. Although the owners wanted the garden to have plenty of greenery, they didn't have time to do too much in the way of plant maintenance. As a final twist, there was a further stipulation: the design had to incorporate their dream luxury item – a hot tub.

This garden would need a designer with plenty of ingenuity, a practical mind to deal with the not inconsiderable problems, and a sense of humour. Douglas Coltart (see Designers' Biographies, page 122) fitted the bill exactly; he is a lecturer and garden designer, and made his first television appearances on the BBC programme *The Beechgrove Garden*. As an added bonus, this multi-award-winning designer is a local boy, who understands the worst of the Scottish weather. Douglas is inspired in his work by his native landscape; his own garden is surrounded on all sides by gently rolling hills. His first thoughts on seeing the roof terrace were how to integrate the distant views of the hills beyond Glasgow and incorporate some of the history of the area. After a discussion with the owners, measurements and photographs were taken and Douglas could begin shaping his ideas into a design.

When embarking on a new roof terrace, the first priority is to have it checked over by a structural engineer. Calculations were made based on the strength of the building, and the

amount of loading it would bear. Douglas could then work out exactly how much weight he could add to the roof. Generally, how the load is distributed is as important as the actual weight – small areas of heavy weight can be more problematic than the same load spread evenly over a large area. In his original design Douglas wanted large, square planters in each corner of the terrace for the trees he hoped to include in the plan. However, these were immediately vetoed by the engineer because they would place too great a concentration of weight on small sections of the roof.

As Douglas was dealing with a listed building, permission had to be sought to develop the terrace. This was granted, with the proviso that nothing be fixed to the side wall of the building, which meant that another part of the original design, a sail-shaped canopy, had to go. But Douglas was undeterred, and after further alterations he presented the owners with a beautiful finished design.

Taking as his inspiration the famous Paisley swirls found in Victorian textile designs, Douglas planned to cover the terrace with contrasting wooden decking, cut and shaped into the curved lines so familiar in Paisley patterns. The widest curve would sweep across the roof, de-emphasizing the rectilinear shape of the terrace. The hot tub was to be positioned near the door that opened on to

the roof from the living area of the flat; in this way it was just a short dash back into the warmth after enjoying a mid-winter soak.

At last, following all the preliminaries, work could commence. The terrace had been covered in dull concrete slabs, and the original plan, and cheaper option, was to build the decking directly on top of them. But weight restrictions meant that the slabs would have to come up. The surface underneath was in good order and the timber frame supporting the decking could be constructed. This was to be a floating frame without any fixings on to the roof surface so that the waterproofing wasn't compromised in any way. The finished height of the deck would be higher than that of the previous paved surface, making the transition from interior to exterior more comfortable. Douglas needed the extra height to allow him to include a water rill in the design.

Left: The graceful curve of decking sweeps across the rectangular space.

Opposite: A collection of contrasting grasses will tolerate the harsh weather conditions.

Introducing water into a roof garden is a delightful idea that is rarely carried out. But if the work is done carefully to ensure there are no leakages, water features really add something to gardens above ground level. The sweeping curve of the rill was constructed below the surface of the deck and lined with black butyl liner. This was disguised with vertical, cross-cut timber pieces, which formed a little dividing wall between the water and the raised planting area. On the deck side an edging of short timber sections was laid along the rill. Simple and stunning light-fittings were installed along the timber edging at regular intervals. These were flush with the surface of the deck and could be walked on.

On the other side of the terrace the same pieces of edging timber followed the shape of the deck. Here Douglas had inserted steel balls into some of the pieces so that half of each sphere protruded. These were painted with silver metallic paint to give a matt finish, and looked like giant ball-bearings. This simple idea gave the design a space-age touch and brought something unique, tactile and playful to the garden.

The centre of the decked area was brought to life by the subtle swirl of the Paisley motif. Douglas created the pattern using the same cross-cut pieces of timber and inserted them vertically into the surrounding

horizontally laid decking. Once complete, the deck was almost too attractive to hide with garden furniture. The hot tub, which had been craned in from the roadside, was installed and, though large enough to make its presence felt, looked integral to the overall design.

Douglas chose to create large, raised planting beds from fibreglass, rather than using individual containers for the plants. This would give the garden a similar look to a ground-level plot. The planting beds were constructed to be deep enough for the roots of the plants, some of which were quite large, to be able to get a firm hold. The base of the beds was given a layer of lightweight pea-gravel to improve drainage, and this was topped up with 6 cubic metres of compost mixture, a blend of multi-purpose and soil-based compost. This last ingredient was particularly important to give real substance to the mix for long-term planting, and to support the larger plants. These large beds would retain moisture far better than small containers, but at this point an automatic watering system was installed to ensure that the soil need never dry out.

The planting in this garden had to fulfil certain objectives. Given the planning restriction on increasing the height of the boundary, it was important to introduce plants that could provide a sense of protection

and privacy from prying eyes, and to choose varieties that could cope with the worst vagaries of the weather. Structural specimens were the first to go in. The only plants to have individual pots were a series of three Japanese flowering cherries. *Prunus* 'Amanogawa' has a fastigiate growth habit; that is to say, it grows straight up in a narrow, columnar shape. In spring the trees will be smothered in pale pink blossom, and in autumn their foliage will turn to shades of gold. Douglas positioned them at intervals along the side of the building, to break up the long expanse of wall, and to give them some protection from the elements.

Bearing in mind the extreme weather conditions, he could then begin the rest of the planting. Two young *Sorbus vilmorinii* trees, related to the British native rowan, were placed, one in each corner on the terrace. Their delicate foliage is composed of small leaflets that allow the wind to pass through easily. With the additional benefit of clusters of deep pink berries that ripen to the palest blush pink, this robust tree is a star performer in any small garden. Continuing the theme of protection, it was Douglas's plan to create a weather-resistant barrier of holly and ivy, which was planted around the perimeter railing. These would also help screen the terrace for privacy, but were shaped to allow glimpses of the canal and the more attractive views. In conjunction with some other tough customers – *Viburnum davidii*, *Elaeagnus ebbingei* and an assortment of conifers – a protective outer screen was formed. Within the screen, a gentler microclimate would allow less resilient plants to thrive. Douglas didn't want his clients to miss out on the 'pretties' that would be impossible to grow without the improved conditions.

Opposite: A young *Sorbus vilmorinii* adds extra height to the planting scheme.

Right: *Hosta* 'Halycon', *Festuca glauca* and *Convolvulus cneorum* stand up to the rain.

A low hedge of *Sorbus reducta* gave added protection to a group of *Verbascum* 'Helen Johnson', the unusually subtle colour of the verbascum flowers picked up beautifully in the soft flesh-toned berries of the sorbus. Douglas's planting scheme was well thought out: he chose plants to create stunning colour combinations, with contrasting and complementary foliage sizes, shapes and textures, and a smattering of scented plants. *Nepeta* × *faassenii* and the fleshy leaves of *Hosta* 'Halcyon' backed a row of tufty *Festuca glauca* planted along the edge of the water rill, to create a bluish-green haze. *Convolvulus cneorum* and *Leymus arenarius* added flecks of silver foliage to an area of deep plummy-red *Heuchera* 'Palace Purple', *Hebe* 'Purple Queen' and *Sedum* 'Bertram Anderson'. (Be warned, though, as *Leymus arenarius* is an aggressive grower, as Douglas pointed out to the owners; an alternative suggestion would be *Salix lanata* or *Lavandula* 'Sawyers Variety'.)

With so many difficulties to contend with, this roof terrace was a tall order for any designer. Rising to the occasion, Douglas produced an impressive design that addressed the problems and came up with practical solutions that also look beautiful. He took as his inspiration the history of the building and the local area. His design is a real garden, not just a collection of pots on a rooftop, and is a masterpiece of soft curves in a hard urban landscape. Finally, his skill in choosing appropriate plants means that they will have a good chance of surviving all that the Paisley sky can throw at them.

As a finishing touch, heavy timber furniture and a patio gas heater were purchased to make the garden fit for the owners' friends. A couple of nights after the garden was completed, the party was in full swing. Gentle lighting illuminated the skein of water in the rill, and most guests enjoyed a leisurely meal, blissfully warm beneath the heater. But a small group of brave souls drank to a successfully completed garden from the bubbling cauldron of the hot tub.

Left: Rectangular, galvanized steel containers mulched with slate are simple and stunning in a modern space.

Opposite: Painted terracotta pots are home to a series of box balls.

ahead – and you can have a constantly changing rotation of flowers, from the earliest *Iris reticulata* and crocuses, through narcissi and tulips to alliums and nerines. There isn't a season that cannot be brightened up with bulbs.

The range of different container types is growing all the time. Nowadays the pot itself is often the highlight of the scheme, with the planting – if there is any – simply icing on the cake. In a very small space just two or three carefully chosen, stunning containers can provide the focal point for the whole garden. There is a style of pot suitable for every type of garden, from the most traditional to the sleekest modern space, and the range of materials is rapidly expanding.

Most familiar is the warmth of terracotta, which is available in myriad designs, from the very simplest unadorned shapes to elaborately decorated urns festooned with swags of fruit and ribbon bows. Don't confine terracotta to traditional-looking gardens; when simple shapes are chosen, it can look just as effective in a modern space. If you want to introduce colour, terracotta and timber tubs are both suitable for painting. Wooden tubs, such as Versailles containers, have been used in gardens for centuries. This is a timeless style, which can be updated by combining the timber with an unexpected material, such as galvanized steel, to make up the side panels.

containers

Roof gardens, like the one in the case study, couldn't exist without some form of container for the planting, but the addition of pots makes any garden seem complete. Container gardening is one of the most satisfying forms of gardening. Creating miniature gardens in a pot is an art in itself, and experimenting with different recipes for planting combinations is infinitely enjoyable.

Above all, container gardening gives you flexibility. You can think long term and plant large tubs with small, slow-growing trees, such as olives or clipped bays. Or you can fill them with annuals, ringing the changes with every season. Small containers are relatively light and easy to move around, so alter the colours and planting combinations whenever you please and you can enjoy a new garden every week. Plant up pots with plenty of bulbs – remembering to think

The ball finials that top each corner of the container can be made from metal too.

Galvanized metal containers have become increasingly popular and are the obvious choice for minimalist gardens. However, they can look equally good planted with formally trained topiary. Many garden centres stock a selection, but for something really original try commissioning your own design. Ceramic pots come in a wonderful range of coloured glazes and textured finishes, but do check that they are frost-resistant and have holes for drainage in the bottom. Concrete is perfect for really solid-looking containers for modern gardens, and is growing in popularity with designers.

With containers it is certainly true that size matters. In small gardens it's often assumed that you should stick to small plants and small pots. But filling a little space with diminutive accessories can accentuate the smallness because it's what your eye expects to see. Better to distract from the lack of area by using a few well-chosen, substantial pieces which give a sense of scale and solidity that will exaggerate the size of the space. If you do prefer to use small pots, choosing one design, repeated in either identical or differing sizes, will help to avoid a cluttered feel.

Planting up containers couldn't be simpler. Place broken crocks over the drainage holes and part-fill with a mixture of multi-purpose compost and soil-based compost, which adds weight and helps to retain moisture. Stir in a few handfuls of horticultural grit and, if desired, some ready-wetted moisture-retaining gel. Position your plants, ensuring that there is enough space between the soil surface and the rim of the container to allow for watering. Fill around the plants with more of the compost mixture, firming with your fingers to prevent any air pockets being left below the surface. Give the pot a really good water and don't allow it to dry out subsequently. Remember that once in a container, the plant is totally reliant on you for its needs. Apart from consistent watering, it will need regular feeding with a slow-release fertilizer. For long-term plantings it's advisable to remove some of the old compost every year and replace it with fresh.

braving
the
elements

The roof garden in Paisley suffered from unpredictable weather, but conditions in many parts of the world make Scotland seem positively balmy. Plants manage to survive in some of the most inhospitable places on Earth. In order to cope with these extremes, an extraordinary diversity of plant life has evolved that is adapted for specific areas. For many centuries enthusiastic plant collectors were mesmerized by the beauty of the plants they found abroad, and, as a result, many thousands of species have been introduced into this country. Today keen gardeners are equally captivated, and determined to include in their own gardens many plants that originated in far-flung parts of the world.

All too often we are seduced by an unusual specimen in the garden centre and, before we know it, it's in the boot of the car and on its way home. More often than not, this turns out to be an expensive mistake. Plants invariably fail to thrive when their requirements are not met. There's more to this than feeding and watering: every plant has physical characteristics that suit it perfectly to its native environment. If we can't provide the same conditions, or at least something fairly similar, the plant will sicken and eventually die.

On the plus side, even if your garden has particularly difficult conditions, there is bound to be a selection of plants that will thrive. The trick is to do your homework before you go shopping, know your garden and take a list of suitable plants with you. Sometimes even a very small garden has areas offering quite different growing conditions, which will enable you to grow a wider range of plants. No matter what the aspect, all urban gardens are affected to some degree by pollution. Some plants are unaffected by this, others yearn for cleaner air. Again, it's a question of being selective.

Town gardens are often fortunate in being sheltered, and can be several degrees warmer than those just outside the city. But coastal town gardens and roof gardens can suffer from extreme conditions just as difficult as those found out of town. There is a certain amount you can do to improve problem sites. Windy and exposed gardens can sometimes be protected with physical barriers, but take care not to create a worse problem, with wind being forced up and over a solid barrier only to eddy around on your side. Planting a screening of plants is often more effective. In this way you form a sheltered microclimate within the screen.

Sometimes it's possible to take measures to protect a plant that might not otherwise survive. Using a greenhouse is one way of manipulating a plant's environment: for example, to overwinter citrus plants that may

Left: The vibrant foliage of *Hakonechloa macra* 'Alboaurea' will thrive on a shady roof.

Right: In the stark beauty of this exposed position, phormiums and grasses can withstand a battering by the elements.

otherwise succumb to persistent frosts. Exotic-looking tender plants can be left *in situ* in the garden and wrapped with horticultural fleece or bubble wrap to protect them from low temperatures. A final top layer of an attractive material, such as a roll of woven grass or willow, will help to stop them looking too much of an eyesore in the winter garden. Glass or Perspex cloches do the same job for smaller plants.

In sheltered town gardens in warmer areas many plants, such as olives, that you would not attempt to leave outside in colder areas, can survive the winter happily without protection. Others need just a bit of help. Dahlia corms can be left in the ground, but as insurance you could spread a thick, insulating layer of mulch over the surface of the soil above. If you leave the tops on perennial grasses over the winter instead of cutting them back in late autumn, they will protect themselves.

Full sun can be a blessing; there is an enormous range of sun-loving plants. On the other hand, you'll miss out on the gentle charms of shade-lovers, and have to deal with all the problems that go with drought. Hose-pipe bans can mean death to plants that are not specially adapted to survive dry conditions. Luckily, there are many that are perfectly content in the sun. Leaf shape and colour are often good indicators of a plant's preferred growing conditions. Silvery foliage is covered in hundreds of tiny, soft hairs that prevent water evaporation and is found on plants adapted to cope with low water levels or well-drained soils. Narrow leaves, such as those on lavender, are also an indication that the plant will tolerate full sun: the reduced surface area helps to conserve moisture. (Shade-loving plants often have large, rounded foliage to make the most of the limited light they receive.) Succulents work in a different way, storing water within their fleshy leaves.

Some of these adaptations are also helpful for plants struggling with exposed, windy sites, which can also quickly have a drying effect on plants. In addition, plants with divided leaves or leaflets are less likely to suffer physical damage in high winds. In coastal areas plants have to cope with drying, salt-laden winds. Tough plants, such as *Atriplex halimus* and eryngiums, are needed here. Nature often provides clues to help you select the best plants for your own garden. A plant's form – its natural shape – is also the result of evolutionary necessity. Low mounded or hummock-forming plants are often simply trying to get out of the wind. Spiky or thorny shrubs may have been fending off hungry herbivores. Growing plants that will thrive in your particular garden conditions, rather than giving in to momentary temptation, is the way to hassle-free gardening and a collection of healthy plants.

Above left: *Fatsia japonica* is the perfect easy-to-grow plant for the tropical look.

Above right: *Canna striata*, *Lobelia cardinalis* and *Dahlia* 'Bednall Beauty' make a striking tableau of contrasts.

Opposite left: Verdant planting surrounds a small statue.

Opposite middle: Gold is the unifying theme in this grouping that includes the spotted laurel *Aucuba japonica* and the bamboo *Phyllostachys vivax* 'Aureocaulis'.

Opposite right: Emerald fronds add delicacy to an exotic garden.

the **exotic garden**

Lack of space need not restrict your imagination. Go where the fancy takes you. If you

dream about windswept beaches, then plan a seaside garden in the middle of the city

centre. Perhaps the deep blue of the Mediterranean sky and the silvery leaf of an olive

tree evoke happy memories. Why not recreate that atmosphere in the suburbs? One of

the benefits of town gardening is that temperatures are often milder and the gardens

more sheltered, enabling you to grow a wide range of exotic-looking plants. So indulge

that fantasy and bring your dreams to your own back yard.

Left: Ferns are perfect to fill the understorey in a shady spot.

Opposite: A dazzling colour combination that really packs a punch includes *Canna* 'Striata' and 'Durban', *Lobelia cardinalis*, *Dahlia* 'Bednall Beauty' and *Lysimachia* 'Firecracker'.

England may be green and pleasant in abundance, but it can also be drizzly and cold, with that distinctive low blanket of thick, greyish cloud, which has been likened to living inside a Tupperware box. Sometimes you yearn to be transported to a hot and sunny climate, with a blue sky that stretches into space. One way of achieving this is to get on a plane and head for the tropics; the other is to bring a little taste of it to your own home.

Turning your temperate garden into an exotic paradise will cheer you on the dullest day and remind you of holidays abroad. But how do you define an exotic garden? For most of us this term conjures up images of palm trees, dense green vegetation and hot flower colours. But 'exotic' can refer to any type of garden in which the planting is significantly different from the traditional English style, and that usually means evoking the atmosphere of a warmer climate.

The lush tropical style is probably the most popular form of exotic gardening, with sales of Tasmanian tree ferns (*Dicksonia antarctica*) and Chusan palms (*Trachycarpus fortunei*) rocketing through the roof. This Amazonian look is typified by the use of abundant evergreen planting, often incorporating architectural plants with large structured leaves that are far hardier than they appear. But exotic can also mean an arid landscape or a dry river bed. Planting spiky succulents,

such as *Agave americana*, and sculptural plants, such as *Cordyline australis*, will bring a suggestion of the desert to the centre of town. The Mediterranean garden is an exotic style that we are more familiar with – by planting rosemary and lavender among gravel and adding an olive tree in a pot you can almost see the azure of a Provençal sky. All these garden styles are achievable in a small town garden; perhaps the best plan is to choose the look that inspires you.

Whichever style you opt for, all exotic gardens have one thing in common: the plants are the dominant factor. The success of the garden will depend not only on design and landscaping, but also on the type of plants that go into it. These are the main elements and will define the feel you are trying to achieve. It's important to stick to the theme of the garden: if you succumb to sentimentality and include *Rosa* 'Constance Spry', you will dilute the overall effect.

Colour is one of the ways to suggest the type of exotic garden you want. The hot, fiery reds and oranges of *Canna* 'Durban' and *Crocosmia* 'Lucifer' or *C.* × *crocosmiiflora* 'Star of the East' are perfect for the tropical feel. Soft blues and mauves and the golden glow of sunflowers evoke the Mediterranean look. Above all, look at the colour of the foliage: fresh, lush greens are the most important component of humid,

jungle-like gardens, and silvery-greys the prime colours of plants from arid conditions.

It's important before you buy a plant that you ascertain whether or not it's hardy in your part of the country. Garden stalwarts, such as *Fatsia japonica*, *Phormium tenax* and hostas, are typical of plants that give the desired exotic effect without needing any special treatment. An urban plot can be the perfect location for a garden with a tropical feel. The climate is usually far milder in the centre of large cities; warmer temperatures and sheltered locations give tender plants a more friendly welcome than the harsher conditions found out of town. However, even this may not be enough to see some plants through a bad winter, and they may need a little extra help.

Wrapping tender plants is the best way to give them the protection they need. Pack straw among the leaves and stems to protect the crown, which is generally the most vulnerable part, and then gently envelop the whole plant in a layer of bubble wrap or horticultural fleece. When in doubt, check the requirements of a specific plant in a good reference book. Small specimens can be protected with glass or plastic bell-cloches. Orange trees and other citrus plants can either be brought into a cool greenhouse over the winter or left *in situ* and wrapped up. Olives should be able to cope with an occasional drop in temperature without being wrapped if the garden is sheltered. In the worst-case scenario, you might need to move your most delicate specimens to a more sheltered part of the garden or a cold greenhouse. Look after your more vulnerable plants carefully and you'll be rewarded with a garden that many visit only in their dreams.

an exotic garden
designed by **Will Giles**

Left: The glorious Abbey Gardens in Tresco – Will Giles's inspirational garden.

Opposite: The back door opens on to a lushly planted scene, with *Dicksonia antarctica* fronds at the base of the steps.

It can be difficult, when your garden is pretty enough already, to alter it just because you fancy a change. The temptation to stick with what you know, the safe and the familiar, can be too strong to fight. But if you do have a burning desire to be surrounded by a completely different atmosphere when you're in the garden, it's time to steel yourself and go for it.

Our small town garden in the shadow of Alexandra Palace in north London was certainly a pleasant spot. Tucked behind an attractive row of Victorian brick houses, with good light and an abundance of pretty plants, the narrow, rectangular plot already had plenty of good points. However, there were some problems the owners wanted to address: the steep steps into the garden were potentially unsafe, an old shed and an unused coal house had outgrown their usefulness, and the storage facilities needed improvement now that the owners' small son was beginning to accumulate more toys. They couldn't wait to replace the tiny, threadbare lawn and crazy-paving path, and create a proper area for entertaining. But the main problem was that the garden simply didn't speak to them. It was uninspiring and average and the owners were bored with it. They wanted instead to be thrilled by their garden every time they stepped outside.

Knowing that you want a change is almost half the battle; knowing what you want to replace it with is the next stage, and putting it into practice the final part. The owners had already accomplished the first stage and they had some strong ideas about the second. Both of them were fed up with traditional English

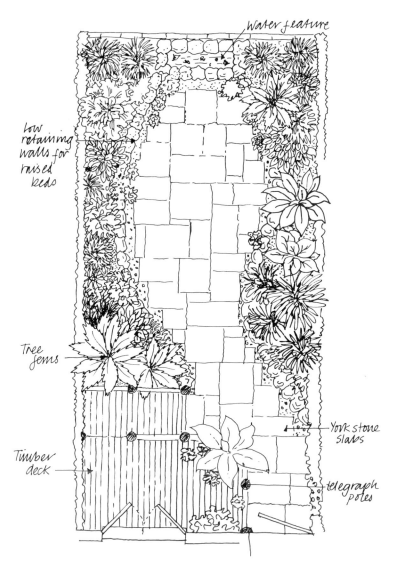

Water feature

Low retaining walls for raised beds

Tree ferns

Timber deck

York stone slabs

telegraph poles

Left: The Abyssinian banana, *Ensete ventricosum* 'Maurelii'.

Opposite: The vertical rock wall forms a dramatic focal point at the end of the garden.

describe himself as designer specifically, though he has created a ravishing, exotic-style garden in Norfolk. He is primarily a craftsman with plants, inspired by numerous trips to far-flung parts of the world, ranging from the Amazon jungle to the deserts of Arizona, and is an expert in how to care for tender plants in a temperate climate such as that of the UK.

However, Will does himself a disservice in playing down his skills as a designer, for his talents are not confined to planting alone, as we were to discover. After a productive first meeting with his clients, and taking careful notes and measurements, Will had some very clear ideas immediately about how the garden might eventually look. Although he admired many of the existing plants, he knew they wouldn't fit into the tropical theme he had in mind, so he advised the owners to give away some of the best specimens.

By the next meeting, Will had devised a simple but stunning design, which, typically – coming from an illustrator – was so beautifully drawn and coloured that it constituted a work of art in itself. Will had paid particular attention to the poor access into the garden: he wanted to provide a platform that people could step on to comfortably from the kitchen. From here you could enjoy a first glimpse of the garden and possibly sit out on balmy evenings. His design for a raised timber deck continued the level of

garden style, and one in particular was a keen traveller who had previously spent much time abroad in warmer climes. She was determined to invoke those happy memories, and the atmosphere of warmth and sunshine that she remembered, in this quiet corner of London. An unusual yet safe water feature was also on their wish list. Thus they reached the third part of the puzzle: how – or more precisely who – could help them achieve that taste of the exotic?

Will Giles (see Designers' Biographies, page 122) is totally immersed in his passion for exotic gardening. His background as an illustrator and his love of plants give him an incredible knack for grouping them together to create stunning planting combinations. He uses the wide variety of textures, colours and shapes in exotic-looking hardy and tender plants to tremendous effect. With customary modesty, Will would not

the kitchen floor directly into the garden, giving a seamless entry into the exotic oasis before you.

Beneath this platform Will had created extra room for storage and taken care to leave clear the entry to an existing storage area under the ground floor of the house, which was accessed by a small door. To add to this rather inadequate space, he planned to make better use of a narrow passageway at the side of the house to store the larger garden tools, barbecue and toys. Feeling the garden needed some sort of focal point, Will decided to build a vertical rockery: this wall would take pride of place at the end of the plot and would incorporate moving water, as the owners had requested. The central area was to be paved to provide a large space for entertaining and tricycle races.

Will's priority when creating this garden was to keep the hard landscaping simple so that it would form a backdrop to set off the spectacular planting to best advantage. The entire perimeter of the garden was to be lushly planted with tropical-looking plants. One of the owners works in lighting design and Will was keen to make use of his expertise in creating the lighting effects for the finished garden. The plan was to illuminate the strongly architectural planting and make the steps down from the deck safe to use at night. Once the design had been agreed with the

owners, it was time to commence work. The dilapidated shed and old coal bunker were the first things to go, and immediately the space doubled in size. Climbers were hacked back, plants removed and the remaining bits of turf skimmed from the surface of the soil. Finally, the site was levelled in preparation for the hard landscaping.

The supports for the timber deck were installed against the back wall of the house. This was constructed using telegraph poles for the uprights and Tanalised wood for the decking and balustrades. The design was for a satisfyingly simple structure with a real feeling of solidity. Generous steps were fixed to the front of the platform and followed the front edge of the deck, rather than going straight out into the garden.

Will had specified York stone slabs for the paved area in the centre of the plot, but cost restrictions meant that a cheaper alternative had to be found. Reconstituted stone slabs in a warm honey tone were a good substitute and worked well with the large quantity of Derbyshire stone that was brought in directly from the quarry for the rest of the construction. The low retaining walls for the raised beds around the sides of the garden were constructed from randomly sized pieces of stone, and the beds were filled with a mixture of topsoil, multi-purpose compost, well-rotted manure and horticultural grit.

Left: *Trachycarpus fortunei*, the Chusan Palm, brings a touch of the tropics to North London.

Opposite: The golden-stemmed bamboo, *Phyllostachys vivax* 'Aureocaulis'.

Concrete breeze-blocks were used to support the stones that would form the vertical rock wall at the end of the garden. Local planning regulations stipulated that a height restriction of only 2m (6½ft) applied to permanent structures on boundaries, but luckily the view over the top of the wall was – for a city garden – not unattractive. The fence on either side of the rock wall was covered with a pair of bamboo screens to provide an appropriately tropical backdrop to the planting. Trellis was used in other places to give uniformity to the boundaries.

Will's spectacular water feature could now be constructed; this was to be the linchpin of the whole design. The rocks were placed randomly one above the other to create the effect of a natural rock-face. Water was to be pumped to the top of the wall, where it had several concealed outlets between the stones. The pressure from the pump was kept low so that the water spilled over the rocks and ran in rivulets down the face, collecting in any small grooves and gullies and creating a glistening sheen of gently falling liquid rather than a cascading waterfall. The water finally reached a large but shallow reservoir at the base, also formed by rocks of varying sizes. Here a range of aquatic plants – such as the tender water hyacinth *Eichhornia crassipes*, which floats on the water surface – would thrive. But planting wasn't restricted to the pool. Ferns and sempervivums were tucked

into gaps between the rocks wherever a small quantity of soil would give them a foothold, and mosses and lichens will doubtless move in before long.

When it comes to plants, Will is a hard man to hold back. He is profoundly affected by places such as the incredible Tresco Abbey Gardens on the Isles of Scilly, garnering inspiration every time he visits the largest collection of exotics in the British Isles, which flourish in the warm Gulf Stream climate. For the Alexandra Palace garden Will had carefully considered the orientation of the plot and selected plants specifically for its sunnier and shadier areas.

The prime position in the shadier section near the house was to be taken by a pair of tree ferns (*Dicksonia antarctica*), one large and one small. These tremendous specimens were planted at the base of the new steps, with a group of hostas at their feet. This gives an instant impression of the exotic as you enter the garden, and your shoulders brush the giant fronds when you descend the steps. At the sunnier end, an enormous 2.5m (8ft) tall Chusan palm (*Trachycarpus fortunei*) had to be dragged through the house before it could be installed in the far corner of the plot. A bank of black-stemmed bamboo (*Phyllostachys nigra*) was planted in front of the bamboo-screened fence on either side of the rock water wall. In this way the

boundaries of the garden began to blur, and in time the mature specimens will completely enclose the end of the plot, while remaining soft and airy in appearance, the foliage rustling with every breath of wind. Among the other structural plants was a second variety of bamboo, this time *Phyllostachys vivax* 'Aureocaulis' with pale gold stems, and the spiky-leaved *Cordyline australis*. An *Aucuba japonica* 'Crotonifolia', one of the common spotted laurels that look so ordinary when planted *en masse* outside blocks of flats, went in opposite the Chusan palm. Here it became a key plant rather than merely background dressing, fulfilling its true destiny by forming a crucial part of an exotic planting scheme.

Beneath these statuesque plants, which created the backbone of the garden, an understorey of rodgersias, ferns – such as *Polystichum setiferum* and *Adiantum venustum*

– and a host of hostas soon filled in the gaps. Flashes of brilliant colour were brought in with the addition of scarlet-flowered cannas, and clumps of mind-your-own-business (*Soleirolia soleirolii*) were dotted among the rocks at the front of the raised beds. A selection of climbers was added to the garden boundaries to increase the impression of enveloping lush vegetation. The vine (*Vitis coignetiae*) and the passion flower (*Passiflora caerulea*) were far better candidates for this garden than roses and honeysuckle.

Will's planting strategy for exotic gardens involves creating a framework of sturdy, evergreen architectural plants, such as the Chusan palm and bamboos, aucubas, fatsias and choisyas. He then uses tender plants, such as codiaeums, to put meat on the bones and add splashes of colour. These are often plants that we would think of as houseplants, but

Will treats them as summer bedding, planting them out once the threat of frost is past and digging them up again in late autumn. In sheltered town gardens, some of the plants that would normally be taken inside can safely be left outside for the winter. Cannas may be left *in situ*, but when the foliage has faded should be cut to the base and the crown of the plant covered with a protective layer of thickly applied mulch – such as composted bark, straw or garden compost – to act as an insulating blanket.

The owners of this garden will probably have to do some basic plant protection each year to ensure the survival of their highly prized specimens. The prime candidate for special treatment is the purple Abyssinian banana (*Ensete ventricosum* 'Maurelii') that Will popped in a pot in the front corner of the deck. This banana is unlikely to overwinter successfully in the British climate and should be brought in for the winter months. A sheltered spot will help prevent the spectacular large leaves from shredding in the wind.

When all the plants were in place, the furniture and containers chosen and the work completed, it was time to road-test the new garden with a special outdoor meal on a late summer evening. With the improved access and plenty of room for people to move around the space – which made serving food and drinks far safer – the garden functioned perfectly. The water-wall really came into its own at night. Small candles were placed all over it, on ridges and under overhangs where the water wouldn't be able to drench them. These sparkled in the darkness, illuminating from behind the glassy water droplets. The sound of the gently tinkling water and the flickering of the flames gave this area a magical quality. This contrasted well with the dramatic shapes and silhouettes of the larger plants, which, when lit from below, gave presence and stature to the garden.

The owners were delighted with their unrecognizable north London plot. The great strength of Will's design was its deceptive simplicity in what was primarily a garden where plants came first. He had succeeded beyond expectation in transforming a dull urban space into a lush, exotic paradise that was full of warmth, atmosphere and, above all, the stunning, large-leaved plants that he adores. It would be hard to find a more dramatic transformation than this tropical oasis in the shadow of Alexandra Palace.

Giles did in his exotic garden, it's often possible to kill several birds with one stone. You gain another point of entry into the garden, a new vantage point from which to enjoy the view, a terrace for entertaining – and some, or all, of the space below can be used for storing tools, a lawnmower and all the children's clutter. Raised platforms in other areas of the garden, and a series of inter-linking raised walkways can also conceal hidden storage areas and are imaginative ways to make the most of the limited space.

Introducing another level in this way can really liven up a dull rectangular space, adding another dimension to the plot. In a small garden the confines of the boundaries are only too obvious, so by changing the levels and introducing extra space in the form of cubed metres, you side-step the restrictions that lack of square metres imposes. But adding different levels to the garden needn't be confined to building raised areas: the alternative is to create further levels by digging down. Some of the best contemporary gardens have had the original ground profile of the space radically altered, yet we are often reluctant to make such a dramatic change.

Gardens on a steeply sloped site are prime candidates for this treatment; slopes are notoriously difficult to deal with and restrict the design possibilities. Far better to cut into the base of the slope and level off the top to

changes
of
level

Town gardens often have a complex arrangement of levels: many have a garden below street level at the front of the house and a plot behind the house at basement level. So, just as Will Giles did in the case study, the first question to consider is whether you are entering the garden in the right place. By creating an additional access from a first-floor drawing-room – perhaps a simple, timber-decked structure, or an elaborate wrought-iron balcony and staircase if the garden style is to be traditional. you might get much more enjoyment from your back garden. Opt for industrial metal grids or rubber floorings to step out into a modern urban retreat, no matter what the date of your house.

Lack of storage space is a massive problem in small town gardens, and sticking an ugly shed in one of the bottom corners is usually the answer. By building a raised platform, as Will

Opposite: Numerous changes of level turn a boring rectangular space into a garden full of structural interest.

Right: The problem of a sloping front garden is dealt with by creating squared-off tiers and planting low box hedges to give a stepped effect.

create two – or more – distinct areas. Even if your garden is as level as a snooker table, you should still consider getting in the digger. Carve out a central recessed section and create an intimate outdoor 'room' below ground level, furnished with comfortable seating, good lighting and a few well-chosen plants.

Altering the level of the planting also adds interest, versatility and plenty of extra growing space in small gardens. Create tiered or stepped beds and plant with eye-catching feature specimens or trailing plants that will drape themselves over the sides of the beds. Even lawns can be split into stepped sections. This is hugely effective but can mean a lot of extra work in terms of maintenance.

When thinking of changes of level, don't overlook the steps themselves. Even the humble garden step can be a distinctive

design statement. There is a vast range of possible materials, styles, shapes and sizes to choose from, but do start with the basic premise that they should, above all, be safe. Reputable contractors will be *au fait* with the dos and don'ts of step-building, and if you plan to build them yourself, make sure you familiarize yourself with the rules too. Don't necessarily assume that the steps have to run in a straight line; it's often far more effective to break up the descent with a series of turns or curves. Steps can also vary in width – though, ideally, not in height – so think of all the possible permutations before resolving what will bring your garden to life.

Left: A mirrored obelisk by
Allison Armour-Wilson
reflects the elegant green
and white planting scheme.

Opposite: Don't be afraid
of colour when furnishing
your garden.

furnishings
and
decorations

The hard work is done, the plot is landscaped, the water feature is burbling and the plants are getting used to their new environment. All that remains is the enjoyable task of dressing the finished garden. This is the time to choose furniture, extra containers, statuary, sculpture and – heaven forbid – gnomes.

The first priority for most people is to be able to start really using their new garden, and this means acquiring some furniture so that you can relax and enjoy that first drink, or get the neighbours over to show off your state-of-the-art back yard. Your choice of table and chairs will depend on space, the style of the garden and the number of people you want to be able to seat. Furniture made from hardwoods, such as teak and iroko, are extremely desirable, if pricy, and weather to a soft silvery-grey. But do make sure they come from sustainable managed sources before you buy: you don't

want to improve your corner of the world at the expense of someone else's. Timber furniture comes in a huge range of styles, to suit everything from the most blowsy garden to sleek modernism.

Wrought- or cast-iron furniture – often in Regency or Victorian style, and usually painted – can work well with formal gardens or those with a traditional feel. Metals are also being used in modern outdoor furniture, though for something really unusual you might have to commission your own pieces. There are many furniture designers who specialize in producing unique outdoor furniture, and some of their sculptural creations are nothing less than works of art. Cutting-edge design is what's required for a state-of-the-art, minimalist urban space, so let your eye be your guide and go as strong as you dare.

There may be extras that will enhance your use of the garden and give you a plot for all seasons and all weathers. If you do have that rare thing, a small town garden with plenty of sun, you may need to invest in a parasol or an awning to protect you from the full force of the rays. Most of us, however, will be more likely to require one of the new gas patio heaters, many of which are free-standing and, depending on size, can be easily moved around the garden as needed. The benefit of being able to extend the long summer days

late into the night and to enjoy Guy Fawkes Night, Hallowe'en and even New Year's Eve outside makes these a worthwhile investment.

In a small space you will probably already have given plenty of consideration to containers, and may have incorporated them as an integral part of the design, but you may find that the finished garden looks incomplete without the addition of a few more. However, avoid the temptation to dilute the style of the garden by importing even a couple of pots that don't tie in with the general theme. It doesn't take much to detract from the design principles that make the garden work as a whole.

Any extra touches are really the icing on the cake. In a small space it's all too easy to clutter the place up with something bought on a whim. If you want to include statuary, one

strong piece will have far more impact if it stands alone. Reconstituted stone is far cheaper than the real thing and, once aged, looks just as effective. Sculpture can bring a garden to life, and is often the inspiration for the whole design, but again, unless you want your garden to be a backdrop for a collection of art, a little goes a long way. Sundials, birdbaths and armillary spheres can all contribute to a small space if placed sympathetically. Mirrored, glass and ceramic objects can be stunning when used sparingly, and for a different look in a formal garden try gilding a simple object – perhaps a sphere – to catch the sun or glow warmly in a shady corner backed by a curtain of ivy.

designers' biographies

On graduating with a degree in landscape architecture, **Douglas Coltart** worked in the private and public sectors before taking up lecturing and freelance design work. His exhibitions and displays at flower shows in the UK have earned him several awards, including two RHS gold medals, two silver medals and two silver-gilt medals for displays in marquees. Douglas's contemporary approach to garden design combines an innovative use of space and materials with imaginative plantings. He set up his own garden design consultancy in 1999, and his work to date includes not only garden designs, but also the design of civic areas and parkland regeneration plans. Douglas is a full member of The UK Society of Garden Designers.

Paul Cooper was formerly a lecturer in art and design at the University of Lancaster and a successful sculptor before turning to garden design in 1984. He has won RHS bronze, silver and gold medals and the Sword of Excellence for the Best Garden at the Chelsea Flower Show. His controversial Cool and Sexy garden at Chelsea in 1994 firmly established him as one of the most thought-provoking of contemporary designers and his innovative domestic gardens have attracted attention for their use of unconventional materials and theatrical effects. He regularly features on television and radio, his work has appeared in various publications and he has written a book, *The New Tech Garden* (Mitchell Beazley, 2001).

Will Giles has been potty about plants, especially exotics, since he was seven. On being told there was no money in gardening, he studied art history and design at Great Yarmouth School of Art and then graduated from Norwich Art School to become an illustrator specializing in botanical subjects. Trips to far corners of the world in the eighties rekindled his love for plants, and in 1986 he was asked to open his garden for the National Garden Scheme. In April 2000 his first book, *The New Exotic Garden* (Mitchell Beazley), was published. He contributes to a weekly gardening phone-in on Radio Norfolk and writes for various magazines and online gardening forums. Ironically, his latest commission is for The Sea Front Partnership in Great Yarmouth, where he is redesigning the Golden Mile, totally in exotica.

Bunny Guinness completed a degree in horticulture and a post-graduate course in landscape architecture, before working for a range of architectural firms and corporations, designing commercial and private outdoor spaces. She then set up her own practice in 1986 and won five gold medals at Chelsea Flower Show (1994–99). The majority of her work is now on private gardens in the UK and further afield, ranging from stately homes to low-budget, inner-city gardens. She has published three books: *Family Gardens*, *Garden Transformations* and *Garden Workshop* (all published by David & Charles). She is a regular panel member of BBC Radio 4 *Gardener's Question Time* and has co-authored a book of the programme (Orion, 2000). She has appeared in several television programmes, including *Gardener's Garden* and Carol Vorderman's *Better Gardens*, where her garden won best garden in the series award, and has her own website: www.bunnyguinness.com.

Cleve West became interested in gardening when injury forced him to retire from a promising athletic career. Taught by garden designer and published author John Brookes at the Royal Botanic Gardens in Kew, Cleve formed his own landscape company in 1986. Since then he has won three RHS Gold Medals and other awards (with sculptor Johnny Woodford) for innovation for his show gardens, has appeared on *Gardeners' World* and written articles for magazines. He now runs his own London-based design practice – where his attention to the use of space is complemented by bold forms and textural foliage offset by seasonal colour – with a separate partnership with Johnny Woodford (Woodford-West) for show gardens and special projects. He also writes regularly for www.dig-it.co.uk and contributes several features on his organic allotment for the RHS's magazine *The Garden*.

Widely recognized as one of London's most exciting florists, **Stephen Woodhams** is quickly gaining international praise for his work in flower arranging and garden design. Having trained at the Royal Horticultural Society at Wisley, where he gained an RHS Certificate with honours, Stephen went on to form his own floral and landscape design company, Woodhams Ltd. He has written two books: *Flower Power* (Quadrille Publishing, 1998) and *Portfolio of Contemporary Gardens* (Quadrille Publishing, 1999); he makes regular lectures and television appearances, and has been featured in many interior and lifestyle magazines in the UK and internationally.

plant directory

Acer palmatum 'Sango-kaku'
Coral bark maple
The young stems of this deciduous shrub or small tree
are bright coral red. The delicate foliage is apple green
in spring and summer, often tinged red at the edges,
turning in the autumn to shades of butter yellow.
A plant with year-round appeal.
Height 6 m (20ft) × spread 5m (16ft)
Sun or partial shade; fully hardy

Alchemilla mollis
Lady's mantle
This perennial has wonderful, softly hairy, rounded
leaves which trap raindrops in their shallow centres. The
frothy sprays of acid-green flowers are borne through
the summer. Remove these before they set seed unless
you want the plant to spread all over the garden.
Height 30cm (1ft) × spread 25cm (10in)
Sun or partial shade; fully hardy

Anemone × hybrida 'Honorine Jobert'
Tall herbaceous perennial with clumps of palm-shaped
leaves towards the base. Sends up slender stems bearing
single white flowers, tinged with pink on the reverse, the
centres with a ring of golden stamens.
Height 1.2m (4ft) × spread 1.2m (4ft)
Sun or partial shade; fully hardy

Asplenium scolopendrium
Hart's tongue fern
An evergreen fern with shiny, strap-like leaves. These
bright green fronds have slightly frilled edges. An
excellent garden fern with a strongly architectural shape.
Height 60cm (2ft) × spread 60cm (2ft)
Full or partial shade; fully hardy

Berberis thunbergii atropurpurea
A deciduous shrub with compact growth and wine-red
leaves. Useful for introducing a touch of purple foliage
to contrast with green-leaved plants.
Height 60cm (2ft) × spread 75cm (2½ ft)
Sun or partial shade; fully hardy

Betula utilis var. jacquemontii 'Silver Shadow'
Birch
This elegant tree is blessed with gleaming white bark.
The foliage colours yellow in autumn before falling.

Stunning when planted in front of an evergreen hedge.
A vigorous grower, so not for the smallest spaces.
Height 18m (60ft) × spread 10m (33ft)
Sun to semi-shade; fully hardy

Cerinthe major 'Purpurascens'
This winter annual (illustrated left, page 125) has
become increasingly fashionable, but it deserves a place
in teh garden simply because it's so beautiful, the leaves
have a glaucous bloom and the pendulous purple flowers
are surrounded by blue bracts. Flowering well until the
frosts, it might self-seed and the resulting seedlings will
overwinter in milder positions. Sow seeds in autumn, or
wait until spring in more exposed positions.
Height 60cm (2ft) × spread 30cm (1ft)
Sun or semi-shade

Choisya ternata
Mexican orange blossom
Reliable evergreen shrub (illustrated right, page 124) with a
neat growth habit and attractive glossy green foliage.
Citrus-scented, pure white flowers appear in late spring or
early summer, sometimes with a second flush in late
autumn. Frequently seen, but no less desirable for that.
Height 2.5m (8ft) × spread 2.5m (8ft)
Full sun or light shade; fully hardy

Corydalis flexuosa
This perennial (illustrated above and left, page 124) is
unusual in being dormant during the summer months.
A mound of delicate filigree foliage appears towards the
end of the year, and in spring and early summer long-
lasting, electric-blue flowers tinged with purple hover
like butterflies above the leaves.
Height 30cm (1ft) × spread 30cm (1ft). Partial shade

Crataegus persimilis 'Prunifolia'
An unusual member of the hawthorn family, this tree has a
rounded shape with glossy green leaves and white flowers in
spring. The foliage turns to fiery shades in autumn, when the
tree is also covered in scarlet berries – the effect is dazzling.
Height 8m (26ft) × spread 10m (33ft)
Sun or partial shade; fully hardy

Crocosmia 'Lucifer'
This cormous perennial is a wonderful foliage plant
with strap-like leaves. The summer flowers, borne on

arching stems, are spectacularly scarlet, though not long-lasting. Best as a large clump within the border.
Height 1.1m (3½ft) × spread 8cm (3in)
Sun or partial shade; frost hardy

Dicksonia antarctica
Tasmanian tree fern
Once a rarity in the northern hemisphere, this plant is now hugely popular. The shaggy, reddish-brown trunk is actually a mass of roots, both living and dead. Large fronds spray out from the top of the trunk in a dramatic fashion. An evergreen in mild climates, perfect for the jungle look.
Height 6m (20ft) × spread 4m (13ft), though likely to be smaller
Partial or full shade; frost hardy

Euonymus fortunei 'Emerald Gaiety'
Compact evergreen variegated shrub. The bright green leaves have white margins and will lighten a drab corner. This easy-going, adaptable plant will even climb if planted at the base of a wall, and also makes good ground cover between larger shrubs.
Height 1m (3ft) × spread 1.5m (5ft)
Sun, semi-shade or full shade; fully hardy

Euphorbia polychroma
A herbaceous perennial with dark green leaves and acid-yellow, long-lasting flowers from mid-spring to early summer. A euphorbia with a neat growing habit, which makes it perfect for a small space.
Height 40cm (16in) × spread 60cm (2ft)
Full sun or light dappled shade; fully hardy

Fatsia japonica
This evergreen shrub is the stalwart of many gardens. The palm-shaped leaves are a glossy mid-green; autumnal sprays of creamy-white flowers are followed by black berries. An excellent architectural plant.
Height 2m (6½ft) × spread 4m (13ft)
Full sun or semi-shade; frost hardy to half-hardy

Geranium 'Rozanne'
This is a brand new variety with a compact shape smothered in violet-blue flowers from June right through to the first frosts; removing the spent blooms will encourage further flowering. This herbaceous perennial spreads but is not invasive and may be grown

in a container. As an added bonus, the foliage develops rich autumnal tints.
Height 50cm (20in) × spread 1m (3ft)
Full sun; fully hardy

Hakonechloa macra 'Alboaurea'
This perennial grass forms rounded mounds of slender golden leaves striped thinly with green. Perfect for adding a touch of brightness to a shady spot. Excellent at the front of a border or in a container.
Height 35cm (14in) × spread 40cm (16in)
Partial shade; fully hardy

Helleborus × *hybridus*
Clump-forming perennial (illustrated right, page 125), hybrid of *Helleborus orientalis* and other species. Excellent plant for woodland-type conditions in dappled shade. Large, long-lasting, leathery leaves set off the saucer-shaped flowers, which come in a range of colours, including white, pale green, buff pink and dusky deep purple, sometimes with speckled markings.
Height 45cm (1½ft) × spread 45cm (1½ft)
Shade; fully hardy

Heuchera micrantha var. *diversifolia* 'Palace Purple'
This clump-forming perennial has deep burgundy-red, heart-shaped leaves, pinky-purple on the underside with a metallic sheen on the upper face. Salmon-pink flowers appear atop slender stems in early summer, but this is a plant grown primarily for its foliage.
Height 45cm (1½ft) × spread 60cm (2ft)
Sun or partial shade; fully hardy

Hosta 'Halcyon'
Perennial with clump-forming habit, grown for its large, overlapping, heart-shaped, grey-blue, fleshy leaves. Understated lavender-grey flowers are produced on tall stems in mid-summer. Although hostas are excellent architectural plants, providing good ground cover, they are also loved by slugs and snails, so they need protection.
Height 40cm (16in) × spread 70cm (28in)
Full or partial shade; fully hardy

Iris sibirica
This perennial is often associated with water, but it is unfussy about growing conditions and copes with well-drained or damp soil. Produces slender, upright

sheaves of foliage and small but show-stopping flowers in rich bluish-purple. A truly elegant plant.
Height 1m (3ft) × spread 10cm (4in)
Sun or partial shade; fully hardy

Phormium tenax
New Zealand flax
A clump-forming, evergreen perennial with strap-like, slender leaves and flowers held on towering stems in late summer. A strongly architectural plant. Many hybrids are available, some of them more compact, with tints of red or gold in the foliage.
Height 2m (6½ft) × spread 1.5m (5ft)
Full sun; frost hardy

Phyllostachys nigra
This black-stemmed bamboo has a clump-forming habit. On young growth the stems are green, turning inky-black after a couple of years. The canes sway and the evergreen foliage rustles in the slightest breeze.
Height 3–5m (10–16ft) × spread 2–3m (6½–10ft)
Sun or dappled shade; fully hardy

Prunus × subhirtella 'Autumnalis Rosea'
Deciduous winter-flowering cherry with a spreading shape. The dark green leaves turn yellow in autumn, after which the tree is periodically smothered in tiny, semi-double, palest pink flowers during mild spells through the winter. Often covered with blossom on Christmas Day.
Height 8m (26ft) × spread 8m (26ft)
Sun or partial shade; fully hardy

Rodgersia pinnata 'Superba'
A clump-forming perennial with dramatic, palm-shaped leaves, which are purplish-bronze when young and deeply veined. The plumes of bright pink flowers are not to everyone's taste: remove them if you think they detract from the foliage. An excellent mid-storey plant.
Height 1.2m (4ft) × spread 75cm (2½ft)
Sun or partial shade; fully hardy

Rosa 'Penny Lane'
Recently introduced climbing rose, named Rose of the Year in 1998. Smothered in nicely shaped champagne through palest blush-pink flowers. Repeats well, often still producing its scented blooms in December. Good disease resistance.

Height 3m (10ft) × spread 2.5m (8ft)
Sun or light semi-shade; fully hardy

Rosa 'Princess of Wales'
Compact floribunda rose, with trusses of pure white scented flowers and dark green foliage. Incredibly floriferous, it repeats well until late autumn. Excellent rose for a small garden.
Height 80cm (2ft 8in) × spread 60cm (2ft)
Prefers full sun or light semi-shade; fully hardy

Sarcococca hookeriana var. *digyna* 'Purple Stem'
Good evergreen shrub for tough places. Tolerant of shade, neglect and atmospheric pollution. The young stems and the leaf stalks on the narrow green leaves are tinged with purple. An understated plant until the winter, when clusters of tiny but very fragrant flowers will scent the garden.
Height 1.5m (5ft) × spread 2m (6½ft)
Full or partial shade; fully hardy

Sorbus vilmorinii
This elegant deciduous tree is a relative of the rowan. The foliage is composed of delicate-looking leaflets that are tougher than they appear and colour well in autumn. White flowers appear in late spring and are followed in autumn by clusters of rosy-pink berries that fade gradually almost to white.
Height 4m (13ft) × spread 5m (16ft)
Sun; fully hardy

Stipa arundinacea
This wonderful evergreen perennial grass forms clumps of arching foliage which change in colour from brown to olive green and rusty oranges, looking good all year. Stems bearing a haze of soft flowers pick up the slightest breeze from late summer to mid-autumn.
Height 1m (3ft) × spread 1.2m (4ft)
Sun or partial shade; frost hardy

Trachycarpus fortunei
Chusan palm
A single-stemmed evergreen palm with numerous fan-shaped leaves. The thick, trunk-like, fibrous stem has a shaggy appearance. Perfect for a touch of the exotic.
Height 10m (33ft) × spread 2.5m (8ft), usually shorter
Sun or dappled shade; frost hardy

Index

Page numbers in *italic* refer to illustrations

Picture credits

BBC Worldwide would like to thank the following for providing photographs and for permission to reproduce copyright material. While every effort has been made to trace and acknowledge all copyright holders, we would like to apologize should there have been any errors or omissions.

The following abbreviations have been used:

GPL Garden Picture Library
HGL Harpur Garden Library
JB Jonathan Buckley
DW Don Welldon
l left, r right, c centre, b bottom

Page 1 JB/Bunny Guinness; **p2** HGL/Luciano Giubbilei,; **p5, 6,** JB; **p7** BBC Radio Times/Mark Harrison; **p8** l GPL/Ron Sutherland; p8 r Clive Nichols/Stephen Woodhams; **p9** l JB/Green & Cade; p9 c JB/Stephen Woodhams, p9 r & **p10** l JB/John Tordoff; **p11** Hugh Palmer; **p13** JB; **p14** l Marianne Majerus; p14 r JB; **p15** l Derek St Romaine; p15 c Clive Nichols; p15 r & **p16** l GPL/Jacqui Hurst; **p17** HGL/Michael Balston; **p18** Colin Philp; **p19** l HGL/Simon Fraser; p19 r GPL/Clive Nichols; **p20** GPL/Michael Paul; **p21, 22, 23, 24 & 25** JB/Cleve West; **p26** l & r Marianne Majerus; **p27** l Hugh Palmer/Colin Livingstone; p27 r Marianne Majerus; **p28** Clive Nichols/Bradley-Hole; **p29** Andrew Lawson/Maggy Howarth; **p30** GPL/Ron Sutherland; **p31** Liz Eddison; **p32** l Chris Maton; p32 r JB/Paul Cooper; **p33** l David Spero; p33 r & **p34** l JB/Stephen Woodhams; **p35** HGL/Luciano Giubbilei; **p36** GPL/Clive Boursnell; **p37, 38, 39, 40 & 41** JB/Stephen Woodhams; **p42** Emap Active; **p43** Marianne Majerus; **p44** Marianne Majerus/Sarah Crisp; **p45** l Marianne Majerus/Bunny Guinness; p45 c Clive Nichols; p45 r Marianne Majerus; **p46** Marianne Majerus/Paul Cooper; **p47** HGL/Lucian Giubbilei; **p48** Clive Nichols/Garden & Security Lighting; **p49** Marianne Majerus; **p50** l & c JB/Paul Cooper; p50 r GPL/John Glover; **p51** l, r & **52** l Marianne Majerus/Allison Armour-Wilson, p52 c Marianne Majerus/David Stevens; p52 r GPL/Ron Sutherland; **p53** Chris Maton; **p54** l JB/Declan Buckley; p54 r Marianne Majerus/Paul Cooper; **p55** Marianne Majerus/Allison Armour-Wilson; **p56** GPL/Clay Perry; **p57, 58, 59, 60, 61, 62 & 63** JB/Paul Cooper; **p64** Marianne Majerus/Robin Cameron Don; **p65** GPL/Stephen Wooster; **p66** Marianne Majerus/George Carter; **p67** HGL/Judith Sharpe; **p68** JB/Bunny Guinness; **p69** l GPL/Juliette Wade; p69 r & **p70** l JB/Bunny Guinness; p70 r Marianne Majerus/Barbara Schwartz; **p71** GPL/Juliet Greene; **p72** GPL/Eric Crichton; **p73** JB/Green & Cade; **p74** Andrew Lawson; **p75, 76, 77, 78, 79 & 80** JB/Bunny Guinness; **p81** GPL/Ron Sutherland; **p82** t Andrew Lawson/James Aldridge; p82 b HGL/Barbara Thomas; **p83** GPL/Steven Wooster; **p84** l Marianne Majerus; p84 r HGL; **p85** l Andrew Lawson; p85 c HGL/Dan Pearson; p85 r & **p86** l DW; **p87** GPL/Stephen Wooster; **p88** Marianne Majerus/Michele Osborne; **p89** HGL/Henrietta Parsons; **p90** Andrew Lawson/Ian Hamilton Finlay; **p91, 92, 93, 94, 95, 96 & 97** DW; **p98** Derek St Romaine/Wynniatt-Husey Clarke; **p99** HGL/Jonathan Baillie; **p100** Marianne Majerus/Ruth Collier; **p101** l Rachel de Thame; p101 r Marianne Majerus/Michele Osborne; **p102** l JB/Will Giles; p102 r Marianne Majerus/Will Giles; **p103** l Marianne Majerus/John Sarbutt; p103 c JB/Will Giles; p103 r & **p104** l JB/Maurice Green; **p105 & 106** Marianne Majerus/Will Giles; **p107** JB; **p108** Andrew Lawson; **p109, 110, 111, 112, 113, 114 & 115** JB/Will Giles; **p116** Marianne Majerus/Paul Cooper; **p117** Marianne Majerus/Jill Billington; **p118** HGL/Tim Ruval; **p119** GPL/Marianne Majerus; **p120** Marianne Majerus/Allison Armour-Wilson; **p121** GPL/Lynn Brotchie; **p123, 124 & 125** Rachel de Thame.